The SENCO as Teacher and Manager

A guide for practitioners and trainers

Frances Jones, Kevin Jones and Christine Szwed

David Fulton Publishers

London

David Fulton Publishers Ltd
Ormond House, 26-27 Boswell Street, London WC1N 3JZ

www.fultonpublishers.co.uk

First published in Great Britain by David Fulton Publishers 2001

Note: The right of Frances Jones, Christine Szwed and Kevin Jones to be identified as the authors of this work has been asserted by them in accordance with the Copyright, Designs and Patents Act 1988.

British Library Cataloguing in Publication Data
A catalogue record for this book is available from the British Library

ISBN 1-85346-713-8

Pages marked with a copyright line are available electronically from the publisher's website www.fultonpublishers.co.uk

Typeset by FiSH Books, London
Printed in Great Britain by Bell & Bain Ltd, Glasgow

Contents

Foreword

SENCOs are a relatively recent phenomenon with a full description and set of roles outlined in the 1994 'SEN' Code. These responsibilities built on work about the role of teachers acting as consultants to colleagues in schools. The mid 1990s was the era of school development plans, 'whole-school' policies and collective 'twilight' sessions. Much of this work showed how a strong subject specialist, particularly in primary schools, could exert a beneficial effect on work throughout the school. It fitted with the burgeoning literature on school effectiveness and school improvement in which the head teacher was shown to have a significant effect on whole-school ethos and thence to attainment levels reached by pupils (and teachers).

However the SENCO is not just a specialist coordinator, akin to a teacher with subject leadership responsibility. The SENCO's role stretches more widely to encompass close dealings with parents, work with a range of services outside the school, representations to school governors and potential legal involvement with appeals or tribunals. The range of skills needed was acknowledged in the 1996 SENTC guidelines about SEN training and subsequently reflected in the specialist standards for SENCOs. OFSTED noted that being a SENCO was a useful career move, particularly in primary schools. For some reason this comment tends to elicit wry humour from teachers.

This book highlights the complexities for SENCOs in taking on the necessary dual child/adult focus and acknowledges both classroom and staffroom realities. These reflect the authors' close involvement with schools. Interestingly, the novel set of demands pushed SENCOs towards a grass roots development of their work. The role has had to be worked out by practitioners, as there was initially no clear blueprint for what it should or could be like in practice. SENCOs have used electronic advice groups (notably BECTA's SENCO forum and the inclusion website), professional associations (such as NASEN) newsletters and journals (e.g. *SENCO Update, Special Children, Special* and *Support for Learning*) to build knowledge, skills and useful networks. It is noteworthy that these developments have been fuelled largely by SENCOs themselves reflecting a democratic and collaborative approach to problem solving and giving SENCOs ownership of change.

This practical book contains many ideas for developing the SENCO's role, both in relation to the promotion of children's learning and as a guide to colleagues. It highlights the many ways in which the SENCO role is becoming both more complex and (potentially) more professionally rewarding. The SENCO is both a manager and a leader. If the SENCO operates as a leader, not merely a manager, this implies a clear sense of direction underpinned by an ability to articulate the reasons for the stance taken. Such leadership demands very high levels of interpersonal skills as well as extensive sound professional knowledge. The SENCO's role, whether with children or adults, is vulnerable to being subject to the latest fads. On what basis can the SENCO decide on one course of action rather than another, and be sufficiently sure about this to convince others of its rightness? Pursuing a succession of tips form various quarters or running with the latest rhetoric-fuelled idea will not, in the long run, be very helpful. The work needs to be rooted in something more solid and this book provides an excellent basis for that grounding.

Professor Ann Lewis
School of Education, University of Birmingham
January 2001

The authors

Frances Jones is Adviser for Special Educational Needs in Herefordshire Local Education Authority. She has worked in special needs in both primary and high schools. She is now an adviser working extensively with SENCOs across the age range in schools and is also currently responsible for the professional development of learning support assistants within the LEA.

Kevin Jones is Senior Research Fellow at University College Worcester. He has worked extensively in the area of special educational needs. He has also published many books and articles in the area, having a particular interest and expertise in behaviour management.

Christine Szwed is Coordinator for Continuing Professional Development at the University of Birmingham, Westhill. She has held senior management positions in both primary and secondary schools and has worked as a senior advisory teacher supporting schools' professional development needs in the area of SEN. More recently she has developed training materials in conjunction with Frances Jones to support SENCOs and learning support assistants across a wide range of schools.

Acknowledgements

The authors would like to thank the many colleagues who have provided support in the writing of this book.

In particular we must thank the numerous SENCOs from all phases of education who have worked with us on our professional development courses in Birmingham and Hereford and Worcester and from whom we have learnt so much.

Thanks should also go to our colleagues who have provided inspiration and ideas for the courses, in particular Dr Jeff Jones, Gillian Tee and Irene Punt (all previously from Hereford and Worcester LEA) and Peter Wakefield, University College Worcester.

We would also like to thank Kevin Rowland (Worcestershire LEA) for commenting on some of the draft, and Louise Bryan for her patience and skill in helping to produce the book for submission.

Our thanks must also go to members of our families for their support and encouragement in getting this into print!

Fran Jones and Chris Szwed,
Janaury 2001

Introduction and ways of using the book

This book reflects the significant shift in the Special Educational Needs Coordinator's (SENCO) role from SEN teacher to manager. Written within the context of the most recent government initiatives it can be used by both SENCOs and by special educational needs trainers and advisory staff. In two parts, Managing learning and Managing people, it explores the range of skills required for the role and offers information and advice in order to develop those skills. Practical activities, which are at the back of the book (and indicated in the text by an Activity symbol [?]) can be photocopied, and downloaded from the publisher's website www.fultonpublishers.co.uk, to enable the user to monitor and evaluate special needs provision in their own schools and to implement a structured process of change in partnership with all those involved in order to improve provision for special education needs.

The following descriptions outline the two parts of the book.

Part One: Managing learning

Chapter 1 The role of the SENCO. An examination within the context of recent legislation and current government policies of the roles of the SENCO, class and subject teachers in assessing and teaching pupils with special educational needs.

Chapter 2 Planning for special needs. The concept and context of an Individual Education Plan (IEP). Formulating and evaluating an IEP.

Chapter 3 Teaching and learning. Analyses the range of learning styles, intelligences and affective factors to be considered in planning teaching which meets the learning requirements of all pupils including those with SEN.

Chapter 4 Supporting progress in literacy. Identifies strategies to enable pupils with special needs to make good progress in literacy within and outside the literacy hour. Suggests way of utilising support assistants effectively.

Part Two:
Managing people

Chapter 5 Managing pupil behaviour. Perspectives on problem behaviours. How to work with colleagues, pupils and parents in preventing and managing problem behaviours.

Chapter 6 Communication skills – giving and receiving information.

Chapter 7 Communication skills – influencing others. Effective negotiation, giving and receiving feedback.

Chapter 8 Communication skills – making presentations. Factors to consider in order to make effective presentations to a range of audiences.

Chapter 9 Monitoring and evaluation. Carrying out effective monitoring and evaluation of special educational needs provision.

The book can be used both as a source of reference and as a training/professional development programme. If the second option is followed there is an Activity symbol in the text which signifies the appropriate place to undertake the suggested Activity. All activities can be downloaded as free accompaniments to the book from www.fultonpublishers.co.uk

PART ONE

Managing learning

Perceptions of special needs have changed rapidly since the Warnock Report (DES 1978). Internationally there is a significant move towards the inclusion of all children within a mainstream setting as an undeniable right. This carries great implications for staff in mainstream schools who, until recently, often regarded provision for 'special needs' as the province of an identified member of staff who often taught the 'special needs' population separately. The 1993 Education Act (DFE) placed that responsibility firmly within the whole-school and the whole staff, giving governors responsibility for the special needs policy and for monitoring its effectiveness. Each school was required to have a designated teacher to act as a SENCO (Special Educational Needs Coordinator) to coordinate whole-school policy and to ensure that children with special needs were taught appropriately across the whole curriculum. The *Code of Practice for the Identification and Assessment of Special Educational Needs* (DFE 1994) contributed the concept of the 'Individual Education Plan' (IEP) which, while outlining individual needs, required management throughout the *whole* curriculum. Thus, the SENCO role extended beyond teaching to the management of special educational needs (SEN) provision throughout the school.

The first part of this book therefore examines appropriate teaching strategies to meet individual and, at the same time, corporate needs against the fast-changing demands of the inclusive agenda with its concomitant implications for teachers' professional development. It explores the complexities of the SENCO's role and responsibilities in relation to those of the teaching and support staff and, in examining a range of learning styles, questions established teaching methods and reflects upon opportunities to develop fresh approaches in order to meet diverse needs within the classroom. Part One concludes with Chapter 4 which focuses on literacy and approaches available to teachers in meeting the needs of children within the literacy hour.

1

Chapter 1

The role of the SENCO

Defining special educational needs has always been an area of contention as there is a powerful argument that we all have special needs of one form or another and that many children will experience some form of special educational need in some subject area at some point in their schooling/education. In any consideration of the role of the SENCO, therefore, the concept, context and nature of special educational needs should be closely examined.

> The concept of special need carries a fake objectivity, for one of the main, indeed almost overwhelming difficulties is to decide whose needs are special and what 'special' means.
>
> (DES 1978, Warnock Report, para. 372)

Warnock envisaged special needs as something a child might have in certain circumstances with certain learning tasks. The concept is fluid, implying that anyone may experience difficulties at some point rather than needs which are owned by a fixed and identifiable group who are in some way different from the majority.

It is clear that, as we move into the twenty-first century with its emphasis on inclusive schooling, the issue of special educational needs has to be considered within the context of changing attitudes and ideologies. It is the intention in this chapter to examine the concept of special educational needs and to consider the range of factors which cause successes and difficulties in learning, while analysing the complementary roles of class/subject teachers and the SENCO. There will also be a consideration of recent legislation and guidance concerning the implementation of the *Code of Practice for the Identification and Assessment of Special Educational Needs* (DFE 1994), the SENCO standards and the revised National Curriculum.

Defining special educational needs

 Activity 1.1 (see p. 102)
Perceptions of special educational needs

According to the *Code of Practice for the Identification and Assessment of Special Educational Needs* (DFE 1994, Section 156) a child has *special educational needs* if he or she has a *learning difficulty* which calls for *special educational provision* to be made for him or her.

A child has a *learning difficulty* if he or she:

(a) has a significantly greater difficulty in learning than the majority of children of the same age;

(b) has a disability which either prevents or hinders the child from making use of educational facilities of a kind provided for children of the same age in schools within the area of the local education authority;

(c) is under the age of five and falls within the definition at (a) or (b) above or would do if special educational provision was not made for the child.

A child must not be regarded as having a learning difficulty solely because the language, or form of language, of the home is different from the language in which he or she is or will be taught.

Special educational provision means:

(a) for a child over two, educational provision which is additional to, or otherwise different from, the educational provision made generally for children of the child's age in maintained schools, other than special schools, in the area;

(b) for a child under two, educational provision of any kind.

This definition can apply to learners with:

- a language difficulty;
- a general learning difficulty;
- a specific learning difficulty;
- a physical disability;
- a medically diagnosed condition with educational implications;
- a visual impairment;
- a hearing impairment;
- an emotional/behavioural difficulty;
- a combination of two or more of the above.

(Hereford and Worcester Council 1994, p. 4)

The SEN threshold statement accompanying the revised draft Code of Practice (DfEE 2000) and the QCA Inclusion Statement in Curriculum 2000 (QCA 2000) mirror the specialist standards (TTA 1999), identifying four broader areas to consider:

- Communication and interaction
- Cognition and learning
- Behaviour, emotional and social development
- Sensory and physical.

Under the 1994 Code definition, 'special' educational needs are relative to the quality of educational provision which is provided for all children within a particular classroom or a particular school. In some classrooms, in which teachers successfully provide for the diverse needs of pupils through good differentiated teaching, children will not require as much 'additional' or 'different' provision as their peers who are taught in less favourable circumstances. Thus, it is possible for a pupil to have 'special educational needs' in some educational settings and not others.

The meaning of the word 'special'

The prominence of the word 'special' at the beginning of the term '*special* educational needs' can have an important influence upon the way in which many teachers, parents and other professionals think about pupils' educational requirements. Many people consider the child's 'special' requirements without adequately relating the word to the other components of the term, i.e. 'educational needs'. Some (e.g. Jones 1992) argue that more appropriate forms of educational provision are more likely to be provided if the words are considered in reverse order (i.e. Needs – Educational – Special), whereby:

Needs   – refers to the learner's all-round needs for security, safety, compassion, to be listened to, a sense of well-being and achievement;

Educational – refers to the learner's rights of access to the breadth and depth of the curriculum;

Special   – refers to any special arrangements which must be made in order to ensure that the learner's 'all-round' and 'educational' needs are met.

 Activity 1.2 (see p. 103)
Identifying the 'special' in special educational needs

Assessing and providing for special educational needs – whose responsibility?

Learning and behaviour difficulties are rarely attributable to single, uncomplicated causes. They are usually the result of a complex interaction of different factors, some of which are easily visible, while others are hidden within the setting in which they occur. If professionals merely seek to identify and respond to the causes which, *to them*, are most visible, they will, at best, produce only temporary solutions to problems (Jones and Charlton 1996). They should be aware of the fact that others (especially pupils and parents) can often throw light upon other causal factors which have an important influence upon learning.

Academic and social learning are affected by a range of factors, some of which reside *within the child*, while others can be traced to aspects of the *curriculum*, or related to conditions within the *learning environment* (Jones and Charlton 1996). A failure to consider adequately any one of these areas, or the interaction between them, is to risk overlooking the very heart of what affects learning for a particular child.

Given the range of factors which can contribute to the learning difficulties which pupils encounter, we need to consider who is best placed to assess and plan responses to a particular pupil's special educational needs.

 Activity 1.3 (see p. 104)
Assessing a pupil's special educational needs – who can contribute?

As Jones *et al.* (1996, p. 129) state,

> The class/subject teacher is in regular contact with the child, has in-depth knowledge of the planned curriculum and can make changes to the learning environment. They are in the best position

to coordinate the planning process. However, while some teachers have the necessary training and experience to carry out this task, others lack the knowledge, experience, or the appropriate attitudes to plan suitable support for pupils who encounter learning and/or behaviour difficulties. The SEN Code of Practice (DFE 1994) sensibly recognises that while the majority of class/subject teachers should be able to determine and provide for the teaching and learning needs of pupils who encounter mild difficulties, many will need to work closely with colleagues and other professionals when assessing and providing for the additional needs of pupils who encounter more serious difficulties.

The Inclusion Statement, within the revised National Curriculum (QCA 2000), goes a long way towards providing teachers with the strategies required in order to meet *all* learners' needs and SENCOs will find this invaluable in shaping support and in-school training for their colleagues.

The responsibility for 'supporting' pupils can be shared in many different ways. The prevailing stress on inclusion strongly emphasises this shared responsibility and seeks to demystify the models of specialist knowledge. Traditionally, learning support professionals have dominated this process, although some have actively encouraged teamwork within the school. Given the fact that all professionals have a potentially valuable contribution to make, each of them must be given the opportunity to describe a pupil's special educational needs as they perceive them and to debate the most appropriate form of provision for that child in the light of their collective contributions. The revised draft Code (DfEE 2000) further emphasises the vital part that parents and pupils must play in deciding appropriate action and in reviewing the outcomes.

For children with more significant needs, when an in-depth analysis of *within-child* factors (e.g. auditory discrimination, visual memory) has been carried out, the class/subject teacher should be given the responsibility (with the help of the SENCO if necessary) for translating the resultant information into practical action in the classroom. This will help the class/subject teacher to build up their own skills in assessing and responding to the needs of pupils who experience learning and behaviour difficulties within their own classrooms.

However, particularly at the 'School Action' stage (draft revised Code of Practice), it will not be necessary, or even possible, to conduct an in-depth assessment of within-child factors for all pupils. In essence the heading 'School Action' demonstrates the draft revised Code's focus upon action rather than assessment. Fortunately a class/subject teacher can circumvent some difficulties (e.g. those caused by poor auditory discrimination or poor auditory memory) without the need for detailed assessment; very few children with special needs will require 'school action plus' (draft revised Code).

While a SENCO, an educational psychologist or a specialist teacher might play a key role in the assessment and planning of responses to causal factors 'within the learner', the prime responsibility for the assessment of factors within the *curriculum* and the *learning environment* should, wherever possible, rest with class/subject teachers in their own classroom, for it is they who are ideally placed to carry out this task. This analysis of needs should be founded, primarily, upon the normal assessment procedures which are used within the school and will then, naturally, inform the planned action for meeting the needs of their pupils.

However, we are mindful, in the short term that many teachers will be unable to do this without the support of experienced colleagues. Thus, SENCOs and/or other professionals will need to help class teachers to develop the necessary observational and reflective skills so that they can recognise factors within the curriculum and the learning environment which might cause their pupils to encounter learning and/or behaviour problems (Jones *et al.* 1996). A number of researchers have drawn attention to key factors which can precipitate and maintain such difficulties, some of which are repeated below:

- a mismatch between the task and the pupil's current level of performance (one study indicated that 65 per cent of tasks were too difficult for low-attaining pupils);
- poor specification of the learning task;
- ineffective time management, thus reducing the amount of time available for teaching;
- lack of appropriate pacing;
- few opportunities to review, revise and reinforce learning;
- the work having an image inappropriate to the pupil's chronological age;
- a lack of 'purpose' in learning activities;
- inappropriate grouping strategies;
- an absence of teaching approaches which encourage independent thinking. (Jones *et al.* 1996, p. 131)

If class teachers and learning support assistants can be helped to recognise those factors which appear to be 'blocking' a particular child's learning, they will then be in a position to make changes to the curriculum or learning environment so that those obstacles can be removed. For example, when there is a mismatch between the task and the pupil's current levels of performance, teachers can adjust the size of learning steps and the pace with which they are introduced, as well as introducing more opportunities for revision.

Pupils should be consulted at each of the above stages. The practice of involving pupils in the determination of their own support requirements has been far from widespread, but is now strongly encouraged in the draft revised Code of Practice. This is important because many pupils will be able to identify areas where they most want to improve and indicate the extent to which a particular form of provision is likely to help them.

Wade and Moore (1993) provide several examples of insightful comments made by pupils, which further support the argument that if they were considered to be 'partners' in the assessment and planning process, their responses would provide a good foundation from which simple changes could be made to overcome, or circumvent, the difficulties which they were experiencing. Jones *et al.* (1996, p. 135) cite a very simple, but powerful example which concerns two partially-sighted boys of secondary school age, who revealed the same worry about arriving late for their next lesson. If they had been encouraged to voice their anxiety, their teachers would have been able to adopt the simple policy of allowing them to leave first to give them adequate time to change rooms. In this case the teachers were simply unaware of the problem, yet the information was easily available.

These simple, but very powerful, insights provide valuable information which could help teachers to make straightforward and effective changes which would alleviate the difficulties faced by pupils. In so doing, they would begin to create classrooms which are much more supportive to learning.

There is now a considerable body of advice which suggests that teachers and parents can usefully work together in active partnership (e.g. Wolfendale 1986, Topping 1991). Jones and Lock (1993) argue that, through the sharing of information, advice and practical support, the resulting assessment of, and subsequent provision for, special educational needs will reach a level which neither the teacher nor the parent would have been able to achieve on their own.

To summarise so far, while support for learning can be conceptualised in many ways, appropriate provision is most likely to occur if the particular knowledge, skills, insights and experience of teachers, learning support assistants, pupils, parents and other professionals are brought together in the planning process. This should involve an appraisal of factors within the child, the curriculum and the learning environment which precipitate and maintain learning difficulties and problem behaviours. To omit one of these sets of factors, or to ignore a key informant/decision maker, might be to overlook significant needs, be they something extraordinary, or simply the implementation of a strategy which opens up learning for more children. Pupils should play a key role in the assessment and planning process. They often have insight into the causes of their problems and can suggest appropriate solutions. We do well to remember that the decisions which are being made will affect their present and future lives.

The pooling of knowledge about the influence of the range of factors which influence a particular child's learning will provide a solid foundation from which to build positive responses to that child's difficulties. These should involve:

- the utilisation of a child's strong learning channels;
- the construction of purposeful learning objectives for that particular child;
- the adaptation of the learning environment so that more effective teaching can be used and blocks to learning removed.

Providing for special educational needs – the teacher's responsibilities

We have outlined the important role which class/subject teachers have in the establishment of high quality educational provision for pupils with special educational needs. Dyson and Gains (1995) highlighted the significance of their role and the expectations which SENCOs should have of their colleagues in relation to child protection legislation:

Hitherto...it has been the rights of teachers which have been protected; adequate provision for non-statemented children has depended crucially on the goodwill of individual teachers and head-teachers; the special needs co-ordinator has been subject to the grace and favour of colleagues, learning to say 'please' and 'thank you' at every turn. The protection now offered to children however, means that the co-ordinator is, for the first time, in a position to require adequate responses from colleagues – and even from heads.

(p. 55)

The role which class/subject teachers should fulfil in relation to children with special educational needs is again set out within the draft revised Code of Practice (DfEE 2000, p. 30, 5.1). The primary class teacher should:

- use information arising from the child's previous educational experience to provide starting points for the curricular development of the child;
- identify and focus attention on the child's skills and highlight areas for early action to support the child within the class;
- use the curricular and baseline assessment processes to allow the child to show what they know, understand and can do, as well as to identify any learning difficulties;
- ensure that ongoing observation and assessment provide regular feedback to teachers and parents about the child's achievements and experiences and that the outcomes of such assessment form the basis for planning the next steps in the child's learning;
- involve parents in developing and implementing a joint learning approach at home and in school.

The same, with age appropriate modifications, applies to staff in the secondary school (draft revised Code of Practice p. 42, 6.1).

The new National Curriculum provides the foundation for the teaching, by *all* teachers, of *all* children, including those with special educational needs. It sets out three principles for developing a more inclusive curriculum:

A. Setting suitable learning challenges.
B. Responding to pupils' diverse needs.
C. Overcoming potential barriers to learning and assessment for individuals and groups of pupils.

The statements are carefully broken down into the detail of the action which teachers should take in order to make inclusion a reality. We do need to recognise, however, the reality of applying these techniques. For instance, examples for C/3a – helping with communication, language and literacy – recommend 'using visual and written materials in different formats, including large print, symbol, text and braille...alternative and augmentative communication, including signs and symbols'. Within this statement there are significant training implications. If teachers are to translate policy into practice, the SENCO will need to support them in identifying their training needs and accessing appropriate training. In doing so, the SENCO might access the skills of special school staff whose developing roles as outreach providers and advisers is highlighted in the Action Plan for Special Needs (DfEE 1998).

Activity 1.4 (see p. 105)
Identifying the professional development needs of the teaching staff in your school in relation to special educational needs

The SENCO clearly has a central role in identifying the key areas for whole-school professional development to support the introduction of the new proposed Code of Practice and the requirements of the new National Curriculum. They will also need to consider the training needs of the school's support staff whose role is becoming increasingly important to the success of the school, taking into account the government's current initiatives in induction training and in working towards providing a framework of qualifications for support assistants. Inclusion means the reality of *all* staff being confident to provide for the needs of all pupils. While the SENCO is the lynchpin in coordinating provision, the whole staff are responsible for delivering the curriculum in ways which will accommodate a whole range of learning styles; these are discussed in Chapter 3. If the methods advocated in print are to become reality in practice, all staff will need to feel that they understand and 'can do' the skills required to fulfil their responsibilities towards pupils with special educational needs.

 Activity 1.5 (see p. 106)
What is the role of the SENCO?

The role of the SENCO

We have drawn attention to the need for teamwork in the assessment of special educational needs and the planning of special educational provision. This has major implications for the role of the SENCO and any school action plan must have the commitment of all staff, particularly the senior management team.

The Teacher Training Agency in *National Standards for Special Educational Needs Coordinators* (TTA 1998) identifies four key areas of coordination:

- Strategic direction and development of SEN provision in the school
- Teaching and learning
- Leading and managing staff
- Efficient and effective deployment of staff and resources.

Recently the TTA have issued guidance on ways to use these standards. We suggest that the SENCO and his or her colleagues use the four key areas of coordination in order to audit the strengths and weaknesses of special needs provision within the school (see Part Two, Chapter 9). From this, the school will identify the areas which need to be developed, using these to inform the school's action plan for special needs. In setting priorities it is important to bear in mind the TTA's key outcomes and to avoid the trap of attempting to change all aspects of provision at once.

It is important to set priorities and identify time-scales in order to achieve change within realistic time limits. The development plan should not be tackled by the SENCO alone, planning for special needs should be a whole-school activity and must have the support of the senior team and of the school governors with whom the ultimate responsibility lies.

Activity 1.6 (see pp. 107–109)
Auditing provision, setting priorities and formulating your school's action plan

Once these areas for development have been identified and an action plan is in place, the SENCO should identify their own:

(a) immediate professional development needs;
(b) long-term professional development needs; and
(c) the professional development needs of teaching and support staff.

The SENCO and the school's senior management team and governing body will need to consider the key outcomes of SEN coordination identified by the TTA in order to identify areas for the professional development of the SENCO.

Key outcomes of SEN coordination

The TTA (1998) advise that effective coordination of special educational needs provision should result in:

(a) pupils on the SEN register who:
     make progress towards targets set in their IEPs; show improvement in their literacy, numeracy and information technology skills; are helped to access the wider curriculum; are motivated to learn and develop self-esteem and confidence in their ability as learners;

(b) teachers who:
     are familiar with and implement the school's SEN policy and approaches to meeting the needs of pupils with SEN; identify pupils who may require special provision, e.g. those with emotional and behavioural difficulties (EBD), and help to prepare IEPs as appropriate; communicate effectively with parents, the SENCO and all other staff with responsibilities for SEN, including those from external agencies; have high expectations of pupils' progress, set realistic but challenging targets which they monitor and review, and provide appropriate support;

(c) learning support assistants who:
     whether employed by the school or the LEA, understand their role in the school in relation to pupils with SEN; work collaboratively with the SENCO, teaching staff and staff from external agencies; through opportunities to develop their skills, become increasingly knowledgeable in ways of supporting pupils and help them maximise their levels of achievement and independence;

(d) parents who:
     understand the targets set for their children and their contribution to helping their children achieve them; feel fully involved as partners in the education process;

(e) head teachers and other senior managers who:
     recognise that the curriculum must be relevant to all pupils by taking SEN into account in the formulation and implementation

of policies throughout the school; understand how best to support those with responsibility for SEN coordination;

(f) governors who:
understand their role in relation to pupils with SEN (and their parents) through the discharge of their statutory responsibilities; develop mechanisms for liaison with the head teacher and the SENCO to ensure that they receive regular updates on the implementation of the school's SEN policy and the outcomes from their regular reviews, monitoring and evaluation of the provision made for pupils with SEN;

(g) LEAs and other responsible bodies who:
receive timely information about the progress made by pupils with SEN, including those with statements; ensure that time spent in the school by external staff is effectively used in support of pupils with SEN.

The Action Plan for Special Needs (DfEE 1998) further identified five priorities for action:

1. Working with parents to achieve excellence for all.
2. Improving the SEN framework.
3. Developing a more inclusive education system.
4. Developing knowledge and skills.
5. Working in partnership for special educational needs.

Clearly, the SENCO must seek to work in partnership with children and other adults in order to promote the progress of pupils identified as having special educational needs and to ensure that all those involved feel confident to participate in the delivery of appropriate IEPs within the context of the whole curriculum. We are reminded that the SENCO should no longer be working in isolation but should be regarded as playing a key role within a team of players which must include not only the education service but other agencies also, such as health, social services, youth services and all those who support special needs.

These recent publications serve to highlight the shift in emphasis in the role of the SENCO. Their skills in teaching are implicitly recognised but, above all, the need for a whole range of management skills is clear. Indeed the revised (draft) Code of Practice acknowledges that the SENCO should, ideally, be part of the school's senior management team if the entitlement for *all* pupils to a broad and balanced curriculum delivered in a way which is appropriate for the range of diverse needs, is to become a reality. The Green Paper, *Excellence for All Children* (DfEE 1997b) reiterates this by arguing that

a SENCO cannot do everything single-handedly. It is the responsibility of all teachers and support staff in a school to be aware of the school's responsibilities for children with special educational needs. (p. 61)

Thus the SENCO is required, not only to possess skills in teaching children with particular needs, but also to have a whole raft of management techniques in order to communicate with and influence partners in action for special educational needs. He or she will need to be sensitive to the learning needs of pupils and the accompanying affective factors and to the anxiety and expectations of their parents. The SENCO must identify the professional development needs of colleagues and support them in overcoming barriers to learning, enlisting the skills of other services and agencies when necessary. He or she must recognise and develop strategies to influence the decision makers in and beyond the school and to activate and sustain changes in perceptions and provision for special needs. Thus, while acknowledging the importance for the SENCO of appropriate teaching strategies, we also consider how the SENCO will effectively disseminate these skills to both teaching and support staff. We will consider how the SENCO can both support and challenge colleagues and managers in order to effect change and monitor the outcomes across the school.

 Activity 1.7 (see p. 110)
Identifying the SENCO's professional development needs

The extent to which successful outcomes are achieved is likely to depend on:

- the acknowledgement by the head teacher and governing body of their responsibility to meet the needs of all pupils which is reflected in the school's policies and practices;
- the way in which decisions, policies and practices, particularly in relation to pupils with SEN, are communicated and implemented throughout the school, including to parents;
- an understanding by all staff that their part in the effective provision for pupils with SEN extends beyond having regard to the procedures of the Code of Practice;
- the assessment procedures and systems for monitoring and recording progress, for example, how SENCOs contribute to the whole-school assessment, recording and reporting arrangements; their expertise and knowledge of the range of SEN. (TTA 1998)

These expected outcomes demonstrate clearly how the SENCO has evolved from a remedial teacher with specific teaching skills to a manager of special educational needs provision requiring a whole range of both teaching and management skills. With the advent of inclusive schooling there are even more implications for the SENCO which reach beyond the confines of the traditional mainstream school and will embrace the whole spectrum of learning needs. The SENCO, while extending and improving his or her own skills, will need to participate in developing the skills of colleagues and to move the whole-school forward in meeting the challenge of inclusion as outlined for schools in the CSIE Inclusion Index (Booth *et al.* 2000). He or she will need to possess the skills both of negotiation and challenge, of conciliation and leadership. Indeed the SENCO's role will not stand still but will continue to evolve as perceptions of individual differences develop and change in the twenty-first century.

Chapter 2

Planning for special needs

The concept of an individual education plan was introduced in the *Code of Practice for the Identification and Assessment of Special Educational Needs* (DFE 1994) in order to ensure that children with special educational needs were appropriately provided for. Its origins may be within the specialised context of a special school or unit and it has proved hard for some SENCOs to marry the concept of an individualised programme with the reality of large groups of children each with an individual need. The draft revised Code of Practice (DfEE 2000) stresses that the Individual Education Plan (IEP) should offer something 'additional to' or 'different from' the differentiated curriculum which should already be in place. This chapter will examine the concept and context of an IEP and consider the roles of those who will contribute to it. The part played by support assistants is examined, together with the management implications for the SENCO.

 Activity 2.1 (see p. 111)
What is the purpose of an IEP?

What is an Individual Education Plan?

The Code of Practice advises the implementation of an IEP for a child who has failed to make progress at Stage One of the Code's procedures (DFE 1994). The IEP should set out:

- the nature of the child's difficulties;
- action
  - the special educational provision
  - staff involved, including frequency of support
  - specific programmes/activities/equipment;
- help from parents at home;
- targets to be achieved within a given time;
- any pastoral care or medical requirements;
- monitoring and assessment arrangements;
- review arrangements and date. (para. 2:93)

The emphasis on the format of the IEP rather than the purpose has led to a plethora of paperwork and the misdirection of the skills of the overburdened SENCO, which does not, as yet, appear to be alleviated by the revised Code. More and more schools have accessed computerised systems with banks of targets which allow a large number of IEPs to be produced hastily but as Gross (2000) observes

> The DfEE's review of the Code promises little. It will maintain the focus on systems which target the individual learner, through an overt, accountable planning system which is inherently and inescapably bureaucratic.
> (p. 126)

It is more useful to focus on the Code's accompanying advice that the IEP 'should build on the curriculum the child is following', and the revised Code allows for more flexibility. Carpenter *et al.* (1996) offer the following advice:

> The Individual Education Plan should fundamentally be an expression of the explicit learning needs of the child with SEN. These needs, however, cannot be addressed in isolation, divorced from the dynamics of teaching and learning that surrounds the child in his/her classroom situation. Targets from the IEP need to be embedded in the regular cycle of classroom activity, married with the learning experience offered to the child through the curriculum.
> (p. 170)

It is vital to embed the IEP within the whole process of teachers' planning and to revisit it regularly in order to evaluate its success in supporting the child's progress. Target-setting may focus on one specific area, most commonly literacy, but must not stand in isolation from the child's daily classroom experience. Byers and Rose (1996) place it nicely in context in their schemes of work process which provides a useful framework for planning holistically and for individual need. Schools are now required to set long- and short-term targets and so the following is an adaptation of their model:

- Policy making.
- Long-term planning.   *Long-term target-setting.*
- Medium-term planning.   *Medium-term target-setting.*
- Short-term planning.   *Short-term target-setting.*
- Recording responses.
- Evaluation and review.
- Assessment and reporting.

The IEP, usually intended for a term, may be incorporated in medium-term planning. Setting targets for the *short-term* can break down long-term objectives into manageable steps for the child. These short-term targets might sensibly be described as a *programme* which stems from the IEP but they would not appear on the initial plan. In the early days of IEPs there tended to be confusion between the two which led to examples being offered by non-practitioners to teachers which were unwieldy and unachievable.

The SENCO Guide (DfEE 1997a) describes a good IEP as one which will:

- be brief and action based;
- indicate the pupil's current level of achievement;
- identify the nature, extent and specific areas of a pupil's learning difficulty;

- specify the learning programme and set specific relevant targets to be achieved, against criteria which acknowledge success, and represent achievable goals;
- specify any other additional support or resources;
- indicate how parents or carers will be involved, and what support or encouragement is being provided;
- include, where appropriate, contributions from the pupil and their views on learning needs;
- detail any additional requirements such as medical or counselling needs;
- set clearly monitoring and recording arrangements with dates;
- set dates for the next review with parents and teachers.

The revised Code (DfEE 2000) emphasises that these targets should be *additional* to and *different* from the differentiated curriculum.

Target-setting does not always come easy and staff will benefit from discussing children's problems together, rather than in isolation. Keep some simple principles in mind and do not let the secretarial demands of the Code take over your life! The following section includes useful guidelines.

- Prioritise. Do not set targets for every area of weakness. When you have assessed the child's needs, decide with him or her, and with other involved adults, what are the most important areas to focus on. You will need to bear in mind not only what is important in your opinion but also what means most to the child.
- Set a small number of targets. Three is usually about the right number but you can vary this one way or the other if you feel it necessary to do so.
- Make targets *brief*, *realistic* and *manageable* so that the individual child experiences success and makes identifiable progress, which will increase confidence and enable the child to take on further challenges. Remember:

  A target should express what the child is aiming to achieve, *not* what the teacher is going to teach.

- Avoid vague statements, particularly adverbs such as: *fluently*; *neatly*; *carefully*, which will make evaluation of success difficult.
- Bear in mind, for the targets, three elements: *a verb*; *a task*; *success criteria*; state what the child will be able to do and how he or she and you will know that he or she can do it.

Target-setting for IEPs

It can be noted (Table 2.1) that the success criteria for James might be judged to be too vague. It is not always possible, or indeed feasible, to rigidly quantify criteria. In this case the teacher and the child need to be clear what 'with consistency' means and the time-span for success needs to be identified.

Example

Table 2.1 Examples of target-setting

	Verb	**Task**	**Success criteria**
Anna	*will read*	*two pages of her class reader,*	*with a 90% accuracy rate every day.*
Sally	*will name*	*three colours: red, blue, yellow*	*correctly, when asked, twice a day for three days.*
James	*will write*	*words containing short vowels: a, e*	*correctly, with consistency.*

A sample IEP for a child in Year 2 appears in Appendix 1. This IEP is drawn up on a pro forma which allows for targets to be recorded together with supporting action (Hereford and Worcester Council 1994). There are a number of formats for IEPs available, including those offered in the DfEE's appendix to *The SENCO Guide* (DfEE 1997a). Some include evaluation on the IEP itself, but the format in Appendix 1 moved on to a review sheet to record the results of evaluation. Wherever it comes, evaluation of the plan is vital in order to agree new targets which develop from initial IEPs.

In the example in Appendix 1 the child's mother and teacher, who was also the SENCO, were responsible for the IEP. Often other adults are involved, including support assistants and support services. To date, few IEPs have included the child as holding responsibility, yet the draft revised Code (DfEE 2000) strongly emphasises the need to involve the child. It is important that the child *does share* responsibility and, wherever possible, is involved in setting targets. It can be difficult for overloaded SENCOs to share decisions, especially in high schools where contributions may have to be collected on paper.

It is also true that senior staff and governors do not usually realise the considerable range of people with whom the SENCO must communicate and the enormous time implications. Activity 2.2 provides an opportunity to identify how planning for individuals might be shared and to demonstrate the communication skills required from a SENCO.

 Activity 2.2 (see pp. 111–112)
Who may contribute to the IEP?

The IEP within the curriculum

So far, individual education planning, has focused on setting specific targets for the child who is supported by his or her teacher, other adults and, perhaps, by his or her peers (in the case of peer reading, spelling, etc.), in achieving those targets. Very often, particularly in the primary school, these targets focus on literacy and sometimes numeracy, and are supported by what might be described as a 'remediating' programme of work devised by the teacher and/or the SENCO with advice from other concerned parties. This programme arises from the IEP and provides the detail of the action required to make the IEP work. It is also important that the IEP lies *within the context of the curriculum* and not in isolation from it. The following questions must be addressed:

1. How can the targets be reinforced across the curriculum?
2. How can the child receive full access to the curriculum?

So, while developing the child's basic skills, how can we ensure that the child is able to understand and progress within all areas of the curriculum? Through the assessments we have made (which have included observation of the child in a range of situations), we know where he or she may struggle, for example in following instructions, reading class texts, recording responses in continuous written form. How can we facilitate learning and progress? There is also a need to be aware of practicalities. In a mainstream classroom where a number of children may be identified as having special needs it is not practicable or necessary for each IEP to detail curriculum arrangements. This being the case, provision for curriculum support *must* be considered within the whole-planning process, particularly at the medium- and short-term stages, as shown below:

Long-term planning   – programmes of study, timing, content.
Medium-term planning – methods, range of teaching strategies including those appropriate for the less and more able.
Short-term planning   – weekly, daily, including differentiated teaching to accommodate range of abilities and needs.

It may be appropriate to attach a checklist, with key curriculum strategies identified, to each IEP. It may be more appropriate to include curriculum arrangements for children with special needs directly in class planning and to make clear reference to it in IEPs. It could also be possible to include planning for *groups* of children which relates to IEPs. The important thing is that we *do* consider the curriculum needs of the child and *do* plan to meet these needs. How this is done depends upon whole-school structures and upon what works for staff and pupils. What *will* be useful is to consult with other SENCOs, to share ideas and to develop and refine a system which works within the school's framework.

The IEP in the secondary school

It is generally recognised that the original SEN Code of Practice (DFE 1994) was drawn up with the primary setting in mind. SENCOs in secondary schools, struggling to embed IEPs within the curriculum, may face the traditional perspectives of special needs as uniquely the SENCO's province, somehow divorced from the subject disciplines encountered by pupils with special needs. Secondary school teachers are still coming to terms with their responsibilities and the need to broaden their teaching to include methods within their own subject which enable students with special needs to understand and to make progress. Perhaps it is particularly difficult for teachers who teach the subject in which they themselves excelled at school to even comprehend why others do not grasp the concepts or apply the skills which they find so easy and fulfilling. There is a great deal of work for the SENCO to do in raising awareness and understanding amongst staff in order for IEPs to have relevance in the secondary curriculum. The draft revised Code of Practice goes further in firmly stressing that 'all teachers are teachers of pupils with special educational needs' and that 'subject teacher planning should be flexible so as to recognise the needs of all pupils as individuals and to ensure progression, relevance and differentiation' (DfEE 2000).

Again, staff need to incorporate into their subject plans strategies to support pupils with a range of special needs. Time spent considering how their own subject demands will affect pupils with learning and behaviour difficulties will make their planning purposeful and appropriate. Where departments address difficulties in relation to their own subjects it is then easier to incorporate support for targets on IEPs. For example, if a student has reading difficulties, teachers need to identify key words within a unit of work, provide these to all students, read, explain and reinforce them through display, revision and recapitulation. Subject-related frameworks for writing provide manageable structures which may be used as models for writing for a number of students in the class. The visual framework can be retained for those who continue to need it, while other students may, in time, no longer require it.

Targets in IEPs in secondary settings again must be manageable within the structures of the school. If they are not, the SENCO must make this clear to senior management and to governors. It must be clear who is responsible for supporting progress towards targets in literacy and numeracy, whether it is the responsibility of the SENCO, the English department or all staff involved in teaching the child. Many secondary schools have a special needs link group and the part which its members play can be crucial in ensuring the success of IEPs. In some secondary schools, departments have each been required to set one department target related to targets determined by the SENCO following consultation. This has made IEPs manageable and relevant to both staff and students and has ensured that departments share ownership of the plan. A multiplicity of targets for a large number of students is beyond the memory capabilities of anyone! Undoubtedly, involvement of the student is crucial to the success of the plan, whether its focus is behaviour or learning. How can an individual achieve targets without owning them or knowing what they are?

Evaluating and reviewing IEPs

Unless a need is of an exceptional temporary nature, there will be a continuum of planning. IEPs will need to demonstrate the steps taken both by the child and by those who support him or her in developing skills and making progress. Effective evaluation of the IEP will provide:

- evidence of progress in target areas and whether targets on the IEP have been achieved;
- evidence of progress within the curriculum – this may refer to other records;

- assessment of continuing or reduced need;
- the opinions of the child and of others involved in planning;
- information towards revised planning.

The *SENCO Guide* (DfEE 1997a) provides a useful checklist to bear in mind when evaluating IEPs:

- Does the school's monitoring procedure acknowledge the links between the written IEP and classroom practice?
- Does the monitoring show the effectiveness of strategies employed so far?
- Are all those involved in the IEP process aware of which targets they are working on and how to record progress against those targets?
- Does the monitoring of IEPs result in action?
- Is the monitoring process manageable?
- Are the roles and responsibilities clearly assigned?

Review of the IEP should incorporate targets which support progress for the pupil. When the child is moving into a new class this means that liaison between staff is vital in ensuring continuity and it may well be necessary for the SENCO to highlight this need and to check that records are transferred and referred to when planning is revised. This is also true for a child who is moving to a new school. When children move schools there are crucial issues of liaison and continuity of understanding and provision for the receiving SENCO to address with feeder schools.

Frequently an issue which arises amongst SENCOs is that of paperwork overload. How can paperwork be refined so that SENCOs spend less time on recording and more on working with the children? When reviewing IEPs SENCOs and class/subject teachers do, at times, conclude that a child may well need to continue to work on, or consolidate, targets, and/or the required action may be the same. In this case, it really is not necessary to rewrite an IEP. With the consent of those involved, it can be photocopied with a revised date, a new date can be added, or perhaps just a part of it needs to be rewritten. This saves time and paper!

The SENCO's timetable over the year must incorporate time for evaluation and review since, again, the process involves a number of contributors whom the SENCO needs to consult. It is worth bearing in mind that, whereas a significant chunk of weekly time out of the classroom may be beyond the budget of a small primary school, identified periods over the year, where time for planning and review are essential, should be possible to accommodate in the budget as long as the SENCO gives the head and governors sufficient notice. In secondary schools, the SEN link team may be the means of collecting departmental contributions towards a review. The SENCO needs to work within the structure of the school and may ask to attend identified year meetings in order to evaluate planning. What you *do* need to consider, if you are a secondary SENCO, is whether your link team representatives can be effective within their departments. The ideal situation would be for those representatives to be heads of departments in which case it may be more effective for the school to identify a heads of departments (HoDs) meeting for the evaluation and review of IEPs where HoDs have previously collated responses to IEPs in order to consult on revised targets and action to support progress. Appendix 2 is a pro forma which may be useful in agreeing, during discussion, where targets can be supported in subject areas. What is really important here is to ascertain whether IEPs are impacting upon progress in the curriculum and, if not, what are *the departments*, as well as the SENCO, going to do about it?

There is no doubt that for the IEP process to be effective there needs to be a clear understanding of responsibilities and a planned timetable over the year to ensure regular and consistent evaluation and review. This will be an integral part of the whole-school planning process and will provide a reminder for those involved in planning of IEPs. It will also demonstrate to senior managers both the time and the financial implications of manageable and effective planning for individuals with special needs. For IEPs to work, they must be recognised as being embedded within the curriculum, responding to curriculum requirements, and to the needs of the indvidual child.

Making effective use of support assistants

Support assistants can play a pivotal role in the devising and implementation of IEPs and there has been a substantial increase in the numbers of assistants within the national literacy initiative, particularly in the delivery of the additional literacy support scheme. They posses a whole range of skills and expertise which the school needs to take into account when planning how best to support pupils' learning. The national standards for SENCOs (TTA 1998) make the assumption that it is the SENCO who will be responsible for support assistants and, indeed, many SENCOs *do* have the relevant skills. In practice, however, many support staff are directed solely by individual class teachers and lines of management are not defined. Where there are a significant number of support assistants within the school, the implications for management skills and responsibility should not be ignored. In addition there is a huge time implication for the SENCO. If you, as SENCO, find yourself responsible for the deployment and professional development of these staff, the school will need to address the concomitant management implications of your role.

Nationally, support assistants are, at last, receiving appropriate recognition and their roles and responsibilities are in the spotlight. The government has developed a 'Teaching Assistant' induction package and is currently developing a training structure which, hopefully, will bring together the plethora of qualifications on offer and provide a pathway towards a teaching qualification. A number of terms are in use to describe these staff. The most common at the present time is 'learning support assistant' (LSA) which, we believe, most accurately reflects their function, and which we will use in our discussion of their role in school.

While many LEAs and further and higher educational establishments are providing training, it is also important that every school is clear about both induction procedures and management structures for support staff. Working with SENCOs and LSAs we identified the following as essential information for LSAs when taking up their role in your school.

An LSA needs to know:

- Her/his job description.
- Conditions of service.
- The school year.
- Timings of the school day.
- All staff and their roles.
- The management structure.
- Her/his own line manager.
- Her/his timetable.
- Timetables of others where appropriate.
- Health and safety procedures.
- Fire drill.
- The school's behaviour policy.
- Grievance and disciplinary procedures.
- The appraisal system.
- A list of governors.
- Professional development (training) opportunities and how to access them.
- What staff expect of them in and outside the classroom.
- Long-, medium- and short-term plans and her/his expected involvement.
- IEPs of children she/he will be working with and her/his expected involvement.
- Information about children she/he will be working with.
- Information about the special needs of pupils she/he will be working with.
- How to support pupils with differing needs.
- The school's policy regarding parents.
- Who to ask for help.

Providing the assistant with a basic induction package, together with clear information as to where further information and advice can be obtained, will ensure that the school has prepared the ground for her or him to take on the demands of the role smoothly and with confidence.

The role of the learning support assistant in supporting inclusion

Increasingly the LSA is expected to be working within the classroom rather than withdrawing children for separate programmes of education. The revised National Curriculum clearly reflects the national inclusion agenda in which the LSA will play a vital part. The following are some of the ways in which the assistant supports inclusion.

Guided by the teacher, the LSA can:

- Observe identified children – their preferred learning styles, their strengths and weaknesses.
- Carry out structured classroom assessment.
- Clarify explanations.
- Support reading of challenging texts.
- Work with the teacher to provide simpler texts and worksheets when necessary.

- Support pupils in making notes (but *not* do it for them).
- Provide alternative methods of recording, e.g. matching pictures, matching pictures to text, sequencing sentences.
- Provide frameworks for writing and recording for those who need them.
- Provide prompt cards for tasks requiring a long sequence of instructions.
- Support pupils in recording homework tasks.
- Support pupils in familiarising themselves with a strange environment, e.g. a new school or location of a visit.
- Adapt the format of a school timetable or ensure that an existing format can be understood and used.
- Help pupils to practise skills which they find difficult to absorb, e.g. in addition to the obvious ones of literacy, moving around a new school, organising their schoolbag, remembering PE kit (but *not* do it for them).
- Help pupils to develop dictionary skills.
- Assist with computer-based programmes and monitor progress.
- Work on differentiated activities with identified groups of pupils.
- Supervise and support practical work, reinforcing any safety requirements.
- Read back pupils' work as a form of checking to enable pupils to identify errors and areas for improvement.
- Record tapes, e.g. of stories and other forms of text, sequence of instructions, units of work, revision texts.
- Word-process pupils' work to demonstrate potential and/or for display purposes.
- Support pupils in developing their own strategies for learning based on identificationn of learning styles, e.g. spellings, times tables, scientific formulae, revision material.
- Feed back assessments, formal and informal, to teaching staff to inform future planning.
- Assist with planning, contributing knowledge and understanding drawn from regular involvement with pupils.
- Contribute specific skills and experience, perhaps, in high schools, by working in one department for all or most of the time.
- Contribute to the planning and evaluation of IEPs.
- Support teaching staff in ensuring that any specific resources and equipment required by disabled pupils is in place.
- Support disabled pupils in moving around the school and in accessing the curriculum *without obstructing the development of independent learning.*
- Support the teacher in implementing IEPs and, in high schools, provide the link support across the curriculum.
- Identify areas for change in IEPs.
- Maintain records of progress of pupils with IEPs.

Much of what has been summarised here is born out by the National Curriculum's comprehensive Inclusion Statement (QCA 2000). While the LSA potentially can promote inclusion, teaching staff need to consider carefully the relationship between their own role and that of the assistant. It can be all too easy to rely upon the LSA to in effect teach a child with special needs, particularly if the child is disabled or has significant behaviour difficulties so that both child and assistant are *excluded* rather than included. Policies and practice should have full regard to the inclusion of the LSA as well as the inclusion of all pupils and there should be a shared perception among the teaching staff throughout the school of the function of the LSA.

Chapter 4 'Supporting progress in literacy' will look in detail at the LSA's role in the primary classroom. The rest of this chapter will focus on the effective use of support assistants in the secondary school.

The support assistant in the secondary school

There is a vast range of knowledge, skills and qualifications among support assistants. A number of them are qualified teachers who prefer to take the supporting role but bring to it a wealth of knowledge and expertise. It is important therefore that these resources are not left untapped and that skills are matched to need appropriately across the whole curriculum. An audit of skills will identify strengths and enable them to be used to full effect. In some secondary schools individuals are assigned, according to their strengths, to particular departments. They participate in subject planning, contributing not only their subject specific perceptions but also their in-depth knowledge of pupils' individual or several needs. Techniques which they successfully employ with one student can be applied and adapted with others. They are able to work with identified groups of students and contribute towards ongoing evaluation and planning for a range of needs.

For LSAs to be used effectively throughout the school day, every subject faculty or department needs to include in their policy and schemes of work their expectations of assistants in relation to the particular features of their subject. How will they function in a science lesson involving significant movement around the laboratory and use of specific equipment involving health and safety considerations, as opposed to an English lessson where considerable skills in speaking and listening and turn-taking are required? What are the different skills of recording and reflection required by different subjects and how can the LSA support pupils in developing these? Subject staff need to identify these requirements and make them explicit in their departmental planning, policies and practice.

It is not always the best use of assistant time to have them always placed with students in the classroom. There may be times when it would be more appropriate for the assistant to be preparing or modifying materials, checking technological aids or working with other students elsewhere. It might be useful to draw up 'dual' timetables so that, if an assistant is not required in one class they can support in another. In schools where assistants are no longer assigned to one statemented student support can be used much more flexibly. Where individual hours are still in place, support amongst a group of students enables the child to develop more independent skills of learning while, at the same time, enabling the sharing of support wherever possible.

LSAs have demonstrated their worth in planning, supporting and evaluating IEPs. The teachers and the SENCO can draw upon the

LSA's knowledge of individual students to identify priority needs. They can help to identify specific subject areas where the student's needs are greatest and contribute information to enable realistic and manageable targets to be set. The LSA may be the best person to discuss the IEP with the student and involve him or her in target-setting and evaluation. It can be difficult for subject teachers to keep track of IEPs and retain the volume of information given to them, and the LSA can share this responsibility thus providing support not only to the students but also to the teaching staff.

Managing support staff

Very often the SENCO manages a number of support assistants. In a large secondary school this is a job in itself. It is an important responsibility and the SENCO should ensure that it is included in his or her job description. The related management training issues for the SENCO will have to be recognised while, in turn, the SENCO must address the training needs of the support team. The range of training opportunities is growing rapidly and, in addition to providing training for themselves, the SENCO will probably find it necessary to investigate the appropriate pathways for LSAs according to the needs and aspirations of each individual in relation to any existing qualifications they may hold. Recent training initiatives incorporate a mentoring system. This is undoubtedly an important feature of successful training for LSAs but SENCOs will need to consider carefully the time implications and commitments and ensure that, if several assistants require mentoring, the responsibility is shared.

Time is an important issue for the SENCO in:

- managing the team, providing regular opportunities to meet, and planning the most effective use of support staff;
- advising staff on the best use of assistants to support the teaching of their subject;
- involving support staff in the planning, implementation and evaluation of IEPs;
- overseeing the professional development of the team.

Support assistants will also need to be aware of what is required of them since this has significant implications relating to their own time and commitment. There are many dedicated LSAs who contribute way beyond their contract hours and it is certainly more difficult today to confine the job within the convenience of the 'school day' as it existed in the past. Investment by the school in effective management of the support team will inevitably strengthen the effectiveness of the school and the ability of all students, including those with special needs, to make progress across the curriculum.

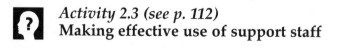

Activity 2.3 (see p. 112)
Making effective use of support staff

Chapter 3

Teaching and learning

A great deal of work has been carried out in recent years into the range of learning styles and the implications for teaching. We often tend to teach according to our preferred learning style. This chapter explores recent theories of differing learning styles and 'intelligences' and offers approaches which go some way towards adapting teaching to learners' needs. By identifying our own and others' preferred mode of learning we can extend and develop teaching approaches. In addition, the impact of the child's self-concept upon both social and academic learning and performance is considered and strategies are suggested to enable pupils to become confident independent learners.

The impulsive/reflective dimension

One dimension of learning style concerns the speed with which one responds to the environment. Some students respond *impulsively* to tasks, whereas others tend to be more *reflective* and to consider various alternatives before responding. Research has suggested that reflective students engage in a hypothesis-testing approach to learning tasks, which is clearly beneficial for most educational activities.

Early research suggested that students who are 'learning disabled' tended to be more impulsive than those who are not (Epstein *et al.* 1977) and a general assumption was made that such impulsivity resulted in increased errors on academic tasks (Walker 1985).

Impulsive behaviours are not limited to students with learning difficulties. For example, many students with emotional and behavioural disorders demonstrate impulsive behaviours as well.

Cognitive mode

Cognitive mode refers to the type of information coding that a student prefers to use. This is also referred to as 'modality preference' and 'spatial-linguistic thinking' (Bender 1995). Some learners prefer to encode memories in visual–spatial terms, whereas others prefer to code linguistically, auditorily. Some of us learn most through the 'kinaesthetic' mode – a hands on approach where we learn through our touching and feeling experience.

If we look at Table 3.1, devised by Colin Rose (1985) (see also Rose 1998), we can judge whether we have a strongly preferred mode of

Table 3.1 Preferred learning styles (Rose 1985)

When you		Visual	Auditory	Kinaesthetic
Spell	*do you*	try to see the word	use the phonetic approach	write the word down to find if it 'feels' right
Visualise	*do you*	see vivid detailed pictures	think in sounds	have few images, those that you do have involve movement
Concentrate	*do you*	get distracted by untidiness or movement	get distracted by sounds/noises	get distracted by movement
Are angry	*do you*	become silent and seethe	express it in an outburst	storm off, grit your teeth, clench your fists
Forget something	*do you*	forget names but remember faces	forget faces but remember names	remember best what you did
Contact people on business	*do you*	prefer a direct, personal meeting face to face	prefer the telephone	talk it out while walking or during another activity
Are relaxing	*do you*	prefer to watch TV, read, see a play	prefer to listen to the radio/play music tapes, CDs	prefer to play sport/games
Enjoy the arts	*do you*	like paintings	like music	like dancing
Reward someone	*do you*	write remarks of praise on their work in a note	give them oral praise	give them a pat on the back
Try to interpret someone's mood	*do you*	primarily look at their facial expression	listen to their tone of voice	watch their body movements
Are reading	*do you*	like descriptive scenes/stop to imagine the scene/take little notice of pictures	enjoy dialogue and conversation and 'hear' the characters talk	prefer action stories or are not a keen reader
Learn	*do you*	like to see demonstrations, diagrams, slides, posters	like verbal instructions, talks and lectures	prefer direct involvement – learning through activities/role playing etc.
Are inactive	*do you*	look around, doodle, watch something	talk to yourself or other people	fidget
Are talking	*do you*	talk sparingly, but dislike listening for too long	enjoy listening but are impatient to talk	gesture a lot and use expressive movements

learning or whether we employ a range of strategies. We can also relate it to the pupils we teach. Many pupils with 'special needs' are quite likely to rely heavily on a particular style and need help to develop other learning pathways.

 Activity 3.1 (see p. 113)
Identifying your preferred learning style

Modality preferences have become associated with the physiology of the brain. Early evidence suggested that in most individuals, the left hemisphere of the brain was the dominant hemisphere for language and sequential thinking, while the right hemisphere was the dominant hemisphere for spatial organisation (Maistervitale 1987). This evidence gives weight to the argument that, generally, boys are more spatial in their learning and that they therefore suffer from the emphasis, in today's curriculum, on literacy skills, particularly in requiring evidence of learning to be presented primarily in the written form (Hughes 1999). Since there is usually a significant majority of boys who are labelled as having special educational needs, such explanations are making more and more sense to those who are seeking to redress the balance of achievement between boys and girls.

Teaching to preferred learning styles

Teachers who are flexible in their teaching approaches and who are aware of these potential learning differences among children can, in most cases, adapt their instructional strategies to the needs of the learner. This is particularly true for children having 'special needs' who may have failed to make progress partly, at least, because of teaching which has relied too heavily upon only one modality. Once we, as teachers, recognise our own preferred modality we can begin to redress the balance for the range of learning styles within our classroom. Taking the model of visual, auditory and kinaesthetic styles, try some of the following suggestions in the classroom.

Visual teaching strategies

- Use colour wherever possible, e.g. for each vowel, spelling patterns and clusters, numbers, categories, highlighting key words and phrases, demonstrating the function of capital letters and full stops. (You will need to check whether any of the children are colour blind.)
- Use icons on worksheets to demonstrate skills required, e.g. spectacles or an open book for reading, a pen for writing.
- When giving instructions orally, support listening with visual information, pictorially or in writing if reading skills are adequate.
- Direct children into groups by using pictures or symbols to identify each group. This can be done effectively by displaying them on a whiteboard where they can be moved around in order to encourage children to move independently from one activity to another.
- Write key words on the board for reference.
- Use blue and black for overhead transparencies.

- Present information in boxes or chunks, rather than unrelieved text.
- Use visual mnemonics, e.g. for spelling write *that* inside a picture of a hat, *then* inside a hen, *train* inside a train.
- Present some information in diagrammatic forms such as a flow diagram, and encourage pupils to do the same.
- Record ideas and planning on mind maps or topic webs. Model the process of recording and encourage pupils to do the same. They can use different colours for each strand of the web to aid transfer into conventional writing if required.
- Demonstrate different parts of speech in a sentence with different colours.
- Use different coloured cards for flashcards.
- Use visual signals to get the children's attention, to signal a change of task or the close of an activity.
- Make use of writing frames so that pupils can see the whole structure of a writing task, understand its purpose and complete the task. For younger children use picture frames, e.g. ladders, balloons, clouds.
- Label resource areas, drawers and trays with pictures as well as writing. Even adults can locate things more easily if there are picture cues.

Auditory teaching strategies

- Use tapes and Language Master to reinforce instructions, provide tasks orally, match sound to letter patterns for spelling, provide practice and build up skills in remembering a sequence of instructions.
- Allow children who struggle with writing to record their ideas on tape then play these back, using earphones, to support their writing.
- Use auditory mnemonics or memory aids for fixing spellings or sequences, e.g. 'oh, you great hairy twit' – 'ought', 'bears eat apples under trees' – 'beautiful'.
- Use stories on tape to support, or as a change from, reading books. This encourages appreciation of literature when difficulties with decoding text can prevent it. Develop a library of taped resources.
- Ensure that children who have intermittent hearing loss can *see* you speaking and that you do not stand in front of a window and block out light while you are talking.
- Check the acoustics of your classroom. If you have no carpet can the children hear you clearly?
- Consciously keep children who may have attention problems on task by using their names to cue them in, e.g. 'Why do you think he said that, Ashley?'
- Ask pupils to retell information and instructions to a partner in order to reinforce and recall learning and fix it in their memory.
- Allow time for pupils who process the spoken word slowly to answer your question. Research shows that teachers generally allow less than a second for pupils to formulate a response.
- Talk through worksheets with children who struggle to read them. Briefly summarise the aims and expected outcomes of the task at the top of the sheet.

- Use oral signals to gain attention, change the task, etc., e.g. 'Freeze', 'Stop, look, listen'.
- Ask your support assistant or helping adult to read back written work to pupils who find it difficult to visually identify mistakes themselves, so that they can *hear* them.

Kinaesthetic strategies

- Demonstrate/model skills wherever possible.
- Demonstrate prepositions like 'up, down, over, under,' as you speak.
- Indicate what you mean by 'left' and 'right'. Be sensitive to the fact that some children will not be able to mirror directions. Use colours if necessary to reinforce left and right on the board and on the page.
- Encourage finger tracing of spelling patterns, sight words, numbers which can be confused, e.g. 6 and 9, 2 and 5.
- Provide plastic/sandpaper/felt/wooden letters for children to experience and feel letters, spelling patterns and words; similarly with numbers.
- Teach through games, e.g. short, whole-class activities carefully timed, commercial games such as snakes and ladders where players can progress if they succeed in reading or spelling a word correctly, pelmanism, snap, happy families using words with the same spelling patterns, crossword games. Use egg-timers and stopwatches to time-limit activities.
- Use feely bags for children to feel and identify letter/number shapes.
- Organise the classroom to permit easy movement between tasks and set up appropriate physical environments for different tasks such as listening to tapes, working in groups, working with a partner, working on their own.
- Use everyday objects to demonstrate in concrete terms and relate to children's own experience.
- Try providing different pencil shapes, grips and thicknesses to suit different writing styles and left-handers. Do the same with pens, providing thin and thicker points. *Do not* insist on fountain pens. Some pupils can write much better with today's roller points, often with quite fine ends.
- Allow familiarity with information technology as much as possible. Often kinaesthetic learners really respond to the keyboard since they remember skills via motor recall and icon recognition.

Always be open to ideas even if they do not suit your own style of learning. They will match someone else's preferred style.

 Activity 3.2 (see p. 114)
Modality preferences and planning provision

The theory of multiple intelligences also has important implications for the planning of special educational provision. Individual learners will have different teaching requirements from their peers according to the profile of their intelligences. Gardner's theory (1993) proposed the existence of multiple intelligences and Smith (1996) discusses

The theory of multiple intelligences

these further, relating each to the context of the classroom. These can be summarised as follows.

Linguistic

Learning through listening, writing and discussion. Responding to the written and spoken word and being keen to develop their own skills in understanding and applying language. Communicating well in written and spoken modes and an attentive listener.

Mathematical/logical

Having the ability to understand and manipulate abstract symbols to represent both concrete objects and concepts. Able to discern patterns, formulate arguments based on hard data, estimate, build models and make hypotheses. Confident from an early stage with the concepts of time, space, quantity, number, cause and effect.

Visual and spatial

Able to visualise easily and have a good concept of self and objects in relation to space. Having the ability to conceive and construct three-dimensional objects and imagine them from different viewpoints. Understanding the effect of mechanisms. Learning through observing and memory mapping with a talent for interpreting and constructing graphs, maps and other visual media.

Musical

Able to discern and experiment with patterns in sounds. Enjoys improvising and playing with different sounds, showing great interest in different forms of music. Demonstrating ability in playing one or more musical instrument with a good sense of rhythm and able to compose music, developing their own styles and preferences.

Intrapersonal

Having an accurate picture of themselves. Being aware of their own thoughts, feelings and emotions and seeking to explain them. Attempting to find solutions to philosophical questions and consistently applying a set of personal values and beliefs. Self-motivated and reflective, utilising journals and diaries.

Physical/kinaesthetic

Exploring and learning through touch, movement, manipulation and physical experience. Well coordinated with a sense of timing and balance and demonstrating creativity through physical movement and expression. Often restless and keen to improve physical performance, enjoying field trips, modelling, building, role play, videos and demonstrations.

Interpersonal

Seeing issues from diverse perspectives, understanding others' thoughts, feelings, attitudes and behaviours and maintaining a variety of social relationships with others. Having an ability to communicate effectively, listen to, acknowledge and respond to the views of others, working well in teams and able to influence others.

Naturalist

Able to recognise and name much from the natural world with an awareness of tracks, nests, wildlife and weather. Having an interest in and good knowledge of how the body works and how to maintain good health. Being interested in global, environmental issues, the origins of the universe and the evolution of life and emphasising the importance of conservation and social issues. (Adapted from Smith 1998b.)

Most of us will relate our own learning styles to more than one of Gardner's intelligences. We can also gain more understanding about the way children in our classroom receive and comprehend our teaching and apply the skills that they learn. Our current curriculum relates to the linguistic and logical intelligences. This can encourage an undervaluing of other intelligences. Although, in the wider society, the interpersonal and intrapersonal intelligences play a vital part, and the world at large has always admired and indeed envied the skills of the artist, musician and athlete without, however, attributing such skills to 'intelligence'. So students who have often been labelled 'special needs' may possess intelligences for which there is little, if any, provision within our education system and may only be able to develop and apply their particular abilities when they escape the confines of the curriculum.

Nevertheless teachers who are careful to deploy a range of teaching styles can do more to harness these intelligences. Many children can learn well visually through the use of colour, pictures, posters, diagrams, mind maps and other visual approaches. Rhythm, rhyme and the use of music (usually baroque is found to be the most effective) can reinforce learning together with frequent modelling and demonstration of skills and hands-on experiences. Many of us learn much more effectively by *doing* rather than being *done unto*. In addition learning is consolidated when children are asked to explain to others what they have learned, for example retelling a story or repeating the teacher's instructions. This can also be a way of providing peer support without threat.

What we have to consider is: *Do I teach as I learn or as others learn?* We need to consciously structure our teaching to recognise and reach a range of styles, to note learning preferences and incorporate these within our range of teaching strategies.

If you would like to explore your own intelligences further, complete Activity 3.3, devised by Alistair Smith at the back of the book and also from www.fultonpublishers.co.uk. Activity 3.4 further examines the implications of these multiple intelligences for teaching. In considering each of the intelligences we are not only helped to adapt our own teaching style to meet the range of learning needs but can also apply this knowledge to improve our interactions in everyday situations within and beyond the classroom.

Multiple intelligences and learning styles

[?] *Activity 3.3 (see pp. 114–115)*
Preferred intelligences

Activity 3.4 (see p. 116)
Implications of multiple intelligences

As well as a consideration of learning styles and strategies it is important to consider the effect of self-concept and self-esteem on learning and behaviour.

Responding to differences in self-concept

A number of researchers (e.g. Charlton 1992) have shown how self-concept can have a marked impact upon social and academic learning. Burns (1982, p. 29) defines the self-concept as:

> the sum total of views that a person has of himself consisting of beliefs, evaluations, and behavioural tendencies. This implies that the self-concept can be considered to be a plethora of attitudes towards the self which are unique to each individual.

As Temple (1996, p. 81) points out, for some children the messages they receive from their experiences are negative and destructive and thus make it hard for them to:

> build a set of beliefs which supports and encourages positive and flexible attitudes and behaviour. These children often expect and invite further negative experiences in schools. They may find it hard to be helped, and adults attempting to assist them may find themselves and their efforts rejected.

Oaklander (1997) lists the following common signs of low self-esteem in children:

Whining
Needing to win
Cheating in games
Perfectionism
Exaggerated bragging
Giving away sweets, money or toys
Attention seeking (e.g. clowning, acting silly)
Teasing
Antisocial behaviour
Being self-critical, withdrawn or shy
Blaming others for everything
Making excuses for everything
Constantly apologising

Fearful of trying new things
Distrusting people
Wanting many things
Behaving defensively
Over-eating
Over-pleasing
Unable to make choices and decisions
Never saying 'No'
Withdrawing
Stomach aches, headaches, vomiting, etc.
Pulling at and picking at themselves timidly.

Temple (1996) suggests that if children are to develop their own positive capacities and act in positive and productive ways, they need enough experience of positive affirming messages throughout childhood about who they are and how to do things. Charlton and David (1996) suggest that such positive affirming messages can be communicated:

- by tailoring our teaching to meet individual needs, and so making success more likely than failure;
- by helping pupils to feel supported and valued;

Often we can achieve this by finding time to listen to them, by learning about and understanding them, by showing an interest in them and by giving them unconditional positive regard (we may not like their behaviour, but this need not stop us liking them).

- by encouraging realistic self-praise;

As we become older, we have to become less dependent upon others' praise. If we are to survive healthily we need self-praise; to tell ourselves that our achievements are something we should be proud of. This practice is an important one in our increasingly selfish society where people are too often unmindful of others and their needs for constant reassurance, recognition and praise.

- by giving them opportunities to recognise, and publicise, their own achievements as well as other positive aspects of their lives;
- by helping them to appreciate that others have feelings;

By doing this we can assist them to socialise more competently, and the worlds of the classroom and school can become better and healthier places to live in.
Finally

- by challenging them (e.g. 'this work is harder than the last piece, but I think you can do it');
- by encouraging them to understand they have more control than they think over what happens to them (this refers to their locus of control).

Responding to differences in locus of control

Charlton (1992) draws attention to the fact that the beliefs which pupils hold regarding the influence of their own behaviour upon academic achievement (i.e. their locus of control beliefs) are crucial in determining success or failure at school. These affective factors are described as follows:

> Internal locus of control beliefs characterise pupils who believe that academic outcomes are dependent upon their personal behaviour; where they desire success they believe it is attainable through their own efforts. Conversely, those who espouse external locus of control beliefs perceive academic outcomes being independent of their expenditure of time and energy and controlled by extrinsic forces such as fate, luck or chance. On occasions when they desire success they remain unconvinced that they are 'masters' of their own destiny. Beliefs of this type often preclude achievement striving and serve only to help to guarantee failure. (Charlton 1992, p. 35)

Charlton argues that an internal locus of control belief is a personality characteristic conducive to achievement-striving and high academic grades and test scores, while externality is linked with inferior grades/scores (Bar-Tal *et al.* 1980, Walden and Ramey 1983).

Teachers, learning support assistants and other professionals should decide whether the learning environment is boosting rather than deflating self-concepts and must consider carefully how to help children to take responsibility for their own learning.

According to Westwood (1993, p. 21), children who experience learning and behaviour difficulties remain 'external' in their locus of control and believe that they are powerless to affect their own progress. They assume that they will fail and that they have no control over this inevitability. Such children need to be taught how to manage their own learning in order to become independent learners. They need help to:

- organise their own materials;
- know what to do when they have completed their work;
- know when to seek advice from their peers or teacher;
- know how to check their work;
- maintain attention to tasks;
- observe rules and routines.

Westwood suggests that children who are clearly 'external' will, at first, need highly structured teaching. If, however, they are placed immediately in very open, child-centred learning situations, the number of occasions when they fail may well increase and their feelings of inadequacy and helplessness will be accelerated. They will need to learn independent self-managing skills gradually if they are to experience success and trust in their own efforts to make progress. Westwood (1993), Charlton (1992) and others suggest such supporting strategies as:

- Simple individual contracts between child and teacher, according to which the child can decide upon the order of tackling new work, how long to spend on it and when to ask for help.
- Self-instruction materials which will help children realise how they can achieve through their own efforts.
- Rewarding success only when the child has made real effort.
- Waiting for children's responses. If the teacher moves too quickly on to another pupil it can cause these children to feel frustrated and useless. They will eventually give up making any effort to respond.
- Encouraging children to analyse problem situations so that they become aware of the influence of behaviour upon outcomes.
- Giving positive reinforcement which identifies what appropriate behaviours are being rewarded.

 Activity 3.5 (see p. 116)
Designing activities to enhance the self-concept

It is clear that the more informed a SENCO becomes in relation to the key areas of teaching and learning the more pivotal they can be in helping pupils make progress. By becoming aware of our own and others learning preferences and by being sensitive to affective factors in children we can support them in developing strategies for learning within and outside the classroom.

Chapter 4

Supporting progress in literacy

In key area 2 of the *National Standards for Special Education Needs Coordinators* – Teaching and learning, the SENCO is required to:

> Disseminate the most effective teaching approaches for pupils with SEN.

> Support the development of improvements in literacy, numeracy and information technology skills as well as access to the wider curriculum. (TTA 1998)

In Chapter 3 we examined the importance of identifying and utilising individual learning styles. Chapter 4 focuses upon the area of literacy and the range of approaches available to teachers in meeting the needs of all children within the literacy hour.

The National Standards for SENCOs identify four key areas:

- Strategic direction and development of SEN provision in the school.
- Teaching and learning.
- Leading and managing staff.
- Efficient and effective deployment of staff and resources.

These clearly demonstrate the shift in emphasis of the SENCO's role to one of teacher *and* manager and the scope of skills required to fulfil the responsibility.

This shift still demands recognition and understanding in some schools, where the SENCO may still be perceived as the 'remedial teacher' whose prime responsibility has been to practise basic skills with children who, for reasons perhaps unexplored, have failed to keep up with their peers. More generally however, schools are recognising the scope of the SENCO's role and the constellation of skills which are required to fulfil it. This development is strengthened by the current national initiatives in literacy and numeracy which patently bring much of what is excellent special needs practice out of the corridor and into the classroom. This chapter embeds its examination of provision for children with special needs within this context, that is alongside their peers and within the National Curriculum. In addition, we will consider the implications of an inclusive agenda for the child, the class/subject teacher and the SENCO.

Special needs in the literacy hour

Activity 4.1 (see p. 117)
Benefits and drawbacks of the literacy hour for children with special educational needs

Some of the advantages of the literacy hour for SEN children can be:

- It provides a structured approach with clearly-defined task boundaries.
- Objectives are explicit from the outset.
- A programme of literacy skills is taught, clearly defined for each year of the primary school.
- In its component parts it embraces the key skills necessary for literacy: text, word and sentence level.
- It provides a range of strategies to enable pupils to understand and do.
- The teacher constantly models successful strategies for the class.
- There are high expectations from all pupils, including an emphasis on pace and challenge.
- It is expected that all pupils are included within the framework of the hour.
- There is an emphasis on explicit classroom management techniques in order to establish appropriate behaviour during each part of the hour.
- It encourages appropriate grouping to meet varying needs and abilities.
- There is a requirement for careful consideration of the range of resources needed in order to deliver all aspects of the hour to all pupils.

During the initial stages of implementing the hour there have also been concerns expressed that:

- Expectations are too high for some pupils who are unable to keep up with their peers.
- Self-esteem and, in some cases, behaviour, is adversely affected by continuing inappropriate demands.
- The shared text part of the hour is too long for the attention span of some pupils who have difficulties with concentration.
- The pace and demands of the word and sentence level parts of the hour are inappropriate for a number of pupils who are unable to match the progress of their peers.
- The structure of the groupwork, in which the teacher works with a different group each day, means that pupils with special needs receive less support than previously.
- There is an assumption that support assistants are available to support the teacher in delivering the hour.
- Where support assistants are used, too high a level of expertise is expected from them.
- The demands of a high level of independent working are too much for some pupils with behaviour difficulties whom the teacher feels require constant supervision.

Despite these reservations the hour does have a great deal to offer to children with special needs and, as staff become more familiar with the framework and less concerned with the time-scales, they are adapting the structure to meet the particular needs of their pupils. For each part of the hour we need to consider what techniques are appropriate in supporting the progress of children with special educational needs.

Supporting progress of children with special needs in the literacy hour

Shared reading/writing

- Always recap on previous learning.
- Ensure children understand objectives.
- Use a child's name before you ask a question to 'tune in' the child.
- Frame questions carefully, stepping up very gradually from closed to more open questions.
- Allow time for children to answer.
- If you are aware that your language of questioning has confused some children, simplify.
- Check that children can actually cope with the size of the text you are sharing.
- Consider carefully the seating of children with attention difficulties, e.g. beside/in front of you/avoiding body contact with other children.
- Positively reward and, therefore, provide a model of, good behaviour, e.g. 'Sarah, I like the way that you are looking and listening really hard.'
- Give identified children a particular task, e.g. holding the pointer, turning the page, showing you where to begin reading/writing.
- Prepare familiarising work with the support assistant to use with identified children, e.g. on subject matter, key vocabulary, understanding, writing techniques.
- Use published or pre-recorded tapes with some children to prepare for/reinforce text.
- Give children with significant attention problems a smaller and/or a shorter version of the text which they may be sharing with a supporting adult.

Word/sentence level

- Give children cards with specific words/patterns/punctuation to look for.
- Actively involve children using a range of learning styles, e.g. use magnetic plastic letters, have children role play words, punctuation marks, letter clusters, parts of speech, use moveable card strips.
- Employ colour to emphasise/highlight/underline phonemes, morphemes, common patterns, pronouns, parts of speech.
- Display key words and consistently revise them.
- Rephrase children's answers sensitively, modelling correct use of language.
- Plan with learning support assistants (LSAs) to carry out preparatory work on word and sentence objectives.

- Make and use moveable punctuation marks, e.g. full stops, commas, question marks, for children to move appropriately.
- Give children missing words/punctuation to place/replace in text.

Guided reading

- Actively develop resources which are at an appropriate level particularly for Key Stage 2 readers with lower reading levels.
- Include reading of plays with sensitive allocation of parts. Some publishers offer plays with differentiated text levels.
- Include the use of non-fiction where pictures and brief summaries significantly aid understanding (applying skills taught in shared text part of the hour).
- Introduce new vocabulary beforehand or with the LSA's support.
- Plan opportunities for preparation/reinforcement with LSAs and/or supporting adults/peers, use of tapes, etc.
- Reinforce learning of high-frequency words.
- Revisit taught literacy conventions frequently to ensure they are fixed, e.g. purpose of texts, author, illustrator.
- Take care that some children are not developing avoidance techniques which are going unnoticed, e.g. visits to toilet, mouthing, distracting attention.

Independent groupwork

- Teach independent skills before groupwork in the literacy hour begins, agreeing rules and teaching signals such as use of alert cards, traffic lights.
- Establish a clearly understood system of signals so that children know when to move to groupwork, teacher work, etc.
- Use a pictorial task board to aid memory and understanding of tasks.
- Plan, with the LSA/supporting adult, extra practice for some children in understanding and carrying out routines.
- Reward successful independent working at regular intervals, ensuring *all* children's successes are recognised.
- Praise more than admonish.
- Ensure children know, perhaps through wall posters or laminated table cards, what they must do before, or instead of, asking the teacher.
- Use an LSA to support groups but *not exclusively* children with SEN in order to encourage independence.
- Give instructions on cards to groups who will have difficulties in remembering a sequence of instructions, with pictorial cues when possible.
- Provide simple written reminder cues, e.g. 'Have you remembered to...?'
- Give attention to layout and text structure of task cards.
- Model, or get your LSA to model new tasks.
- Provide prompt sheets and writing frameworks differentiated for ability if necessary.
- Ensure frameworks are manageable, e.g. smaller spaces for children who need them.

- Provide activities as alternatives to writing, e.g. sequencing cards, manipulating plastic letters, tapes, computer programs, storyboards, games.
- Give identified children responsibilities of ensuring all necessary materials are available, being timekeepers, etc.
- Plan for short chunks of activities for children with limited concentration skills.
- Offer choices to children with behaviour difficulties, e.g. 'You need to choose whether to finish your work now or at lunchtime.'
- Provide a cooling off area for children who may have difficulties with interaction with peers to use at crisis times.

Plenary

- Give identified children specific questions on cards to ask presenters.
- Give some children cards with positive feedback, e.g. 'I liked the way that you ...'.
- Reward appropriate turn-taking. Perhaps use a teddy or other appropriate object to cue in.
- In groupwork prepare children, who may be reticent to feed back, e.g. rehearse responses with LSA.
- Allow children to report in pairs, ensuring that both participate.
- Encourage use of visual aids for children with expressive difficulties.
- Consider encouraging children to use puppets if this promotes confidence.
- Reward, with positive praise, children who achieve their IEP targets, e.g. not having asked the teacher for help during groupwork, sitting without fidgeting for ten minutes, writing with correct use of capital letters and full stops.

Working with LSAs to support progress in literacy

Most schools now employ LSAs; very often in primary schools they support staff and children in the literacy hour. In secondary school much of their work, although often more generally spread across the curriculum, still supports literacy skills. This section, while concentrating on literacy in the primary school, still offers useful approaches for use in the secondary school. Additional approaches for supporting students of secondary school age are described in Chapter 2 'Planning for special needs'.

Activity 4.2 (see p. 118)
Deployment of the LSA within the literacy hour

As with the teacher's role, we will consider that of the LSA within each part of the literacy hour. It is important that LSAs are involved in planning the hour and that they are aware of, and understand, the objectives. This is something which staff need to consider very carefully; it is not just a question of involving LSAs in working with the class teacher but also of providing training for them to ensure that they understand the context of the hour, its purpose and the skills required to ensure success. Support staff who are delivering the Additional Literacy Strategy (DfEE 1999) have already been trained in the appropriate skills and newly-appointed assistants designated by the DfEE as 'Teaching Assistants' are receiving training in the aims and framework of the Literacy Strategy. In addition, support assistants, including those who are employed to support individual children who usually have statements of special educational need, need to understand the emphasis, within the literacy hour, upon independent learning. This necessitates careful planning of support which, while enabling children with special needs to understand and carry out tasks, avoids over-dependence upon supporting adults and promotes learning autonomy. The class teacher needs to monitor support carefully in order to be sure that it is the child and not the adult who has carried out the task.

Shared reading/writing
The LSA can:

- Practise and develop appropriate listening skills with identified children.
- Observe children with special needs to advise on appropriate seating arrangements, attention span, successful strategies for gaining and keeping attention.
- Identify children who may be struggling with language structure, vocabulary, etc., in order to inform future planning.
- Identify children who are struggling to read aloud with the class/are making good progress in reading with the class.
- Under the teacher's direction, prepare differentiated material such as smaller versions of the text, writing frameworks.
- Prepare or follow up a shared text for reading or writing with an identified group in order to promote confidence and practise skills of listening and responding.
- If deemed necessary, carry out a parallel session with an identified group, preferably in, rather than outside, the classroom.

Groupwork
The LSA can:

- Prepare material with the teacher to support group activities.
- Practise skills with children of moving quietly between tasks. Support organised class movement.
- Work with an identified group to find key points and carry out tasks. Make sure the group is not always the less able children.
- Practise, with identified children, the skills which are required within the hour, e.g. identifying key words, specific writing skills, identifying letter patterns and clusters and word families, reflecting on meaning, inference.
- Consolidate key points arising in the shared reading and writing sessions.
- Where appropriate, work on relevant structured programmes with identified children.
- Under the teacher's direction, plan tasks and prepare supporting material for children who are working towards IEP targets.

- Identify where IEP targets can be grouped together to facilitate group rather than individualised work.
- Where appropriate, work on differentiated tasks for writing, e.g. simplified frameworks, reinforcement of writing skills, handwriting skills.
- Identify where children are struggling/making good progress in order to inform planning.

Plenary

The LSA can:

- Help children to prepare presentations for the plenary.
- Practise, with identified children, effective speaking and listening skills.
- Identify children who are struggling to contribute/have become more confident in contributing.
- Revise the content and objectives of the hour with children in order to prepare them for the plenary and to assist them in contributing to it.
- Encourage less confident children to contribute.
- With the teacher, recognise success and praise progress and achievement.

The Additional Literacy Strategy (DfEE 1999) also has much to offer for the work of the LSA. But a word of warning here; it is very phonics-based and if this is where children have a weakness it can be very demoralising for them to be immersed in phonics where they may constantly experience failure. We refer you back to Chapter 3 on teaching and learning needs and to the need for a balance of teaching and support which, while strengthening weaknesses, also capitalises on a child's learning style. While there is scope for argument here, it would be a retrograde step if the sensible range of teaching strategies which are used within the literacy hour were abandoned in the name of phonics.

Supporting the individual reader

Many teachers have expressed concern that the format of the literacy hour does not allow for individualised reading support. The proponents of the hour argue that 'hearing' a child read does not automatically promote the development and improvement of the *skills* of reading. If your school does retain time to read with individuals it is vital that assessment of the child's reading strategies is carried out through a simple miscue analysis and that this forms the basis of support to the child. It is also important to employ a variety of approaches in helping children to develop a range of reading strategies. The general approaches contained in the literacy hour are, of course, also appropriate for the teacher or supporter to use for individuals. We have selected some of the methods which have proved to be particularly effective for individual support and have listed them under the headings used in the searchlight model of the hour.

Phonics: problems with sounds

Children may lack confidence in identifying and blending phonemes and syllables.

1. Look out for regular confusion of some sounds which may indicate past or current hearing and/or speech difficulties, e.g. vowel confusions such as: a/e, e/i, consonant confusions such as d/t, c/t, b/p, m/n, l/y. The 'dark' sounds – 'r', 'n' and 'l' – can also cause problems arising from a history of intermittent hearing loss. The child may have had difficulty in hearing these sounds. You may need to concentrate on their visual representation rather than the auditory one.
2. Encourage identification of onset and rime. Concentrate on the part which is causing the problem. Encourage blending of onset and rime and relate to familiar letter patterns.
3. Develop knowledge and awareness of the link between rime and rhyme by reading stories which contain rhymes, blocking out rhyming words to encourage prediction.
4. Use syllabication techniques – breaking words into chunks – to make them manageable. Make sure the child knows that each syllable should contain at least one vowel and can contain more than one. Build up syllables in words. (Be aware that short-term memory problems can mean that the child has forgotten the first syllable by the time he or she has identified the last one in a multi-syllabic word.)
5. Reinforce knowledge of vowels. Each single vowel can usually be pronounced in one of two ways – 'short' or 'long' (you may use different descriptors). Encourage the child to feel confident in trying both pronunciations.

Word recognition and graphic knowledge: problems with visual representation

Children may substitute a familiar word for a word they do not immediately recognise. The may identify the initial sounds accurately but have difficulty with the end, or, particularly, the middle, of words.

1. Be aware of indications of visual stress such as: often losing his/her place; missing out words; ignoring punctuation; rubbing his/her eyes; yawning frequently. Parents and carers at home will need to be made aware that the child will respond better to short bursts rather than protracted periods of reading practice.
2. Encourage the child to use a marker. Some older students and, indeed, adults still find it helpful to do this. Coloured overlays may be helpful.
3. If initial sounds are accurate, concentrate on the rime and relate to patterns in familiar words.
4. If the problem is with the medial letters, concentrate on these together with the sense of what the child is reading, e.g. horse/house? head, hand?
5. Draw attention to word families and words within words, e.g. sign, design, resign.
6. Use games like pelmanism, snap, to reinforce recognition. The Additional Literacy Strategy (DfEE 1999) has some excellent ideas for games.

Grammatical knowledge: knowledge of context

1. If the child uses the correct part of speech, e.g. 'he wanted the ball' rather than 'he hit the ball' recognise this positive strategy and draw attention to meaning.
2. If the child uses an incorrect part of speech, again concentrate on meaning. Understanding what a sentence contains will help to tackle this.
3. Do not discourage the child from using cues from pictures and diagrams as long as there is not over-reliance on this strategy.
4. Ask the child whether the word he/she is offering makes sense.
5. Draw attention to what comes before and after the word to encourage prediction. Encourage the use of onset to aid prediction.
6. Encourage the child to re-read and give him/her *plenty* of time.

Additional approaches

Motivation is so important for children who struggle to read or who are reluctant readers. Be flexible with reading material. It is so important that these children read text which holds interest for them even if it is not always of the quality you might wish. Bear in mind the following:

1. Adventure games on disk which contain plenty of text. There are also books which use this approach, with short sections of text leading to alternative choices of further short sections of text.
2. Magazines, manuals and information books about their own interests. Remember these may not be to your taste but can be crucial motivators.
3. Taped versions with the text, and sometimes without, to encourage fluency and enjoyment. Develop a substantial library of tapes to support texts.
4. The repeated reading approach – similar to paired reading but using a tape of the story which the child controls at his/her own pace.

Build up a bank of games which will develop sight reading skills and also support spelling. This is another area where LSA support can be invaluable.

Summary

By drawing upon a whole range of teaching approaches in planning the literacy hour and actively involving the LSA, both in supporting the delivery of the hour and ensuring that targets on IEPs are reached, the teacher can identify and meet the diverse learning needs of the children in their class. Many of the approaches stem from good practice for special needs while the structure of the hour provides a secure framework for children with learning difficulties. Strategies used here can be applied throughout the curriculum and, as the strategy reaches the secondary school, 'special needs' may be recognised as 'individual needs' with teaching matching the range of learning styles previously identified.

PART TWO

Managing people

It is interesting to note that much of the literature aimed at supporting special needs provision in schools is related in the main to 'curricular initiatives'. With the creation of the SENCO standards it is clear that a crucial part of the role is concerned with leading and managing staff (Standard C) (TTA 1998). It is this area that the second part of this book aims to consider and support.

Before the introduction of the standards many commentators had noted the increasing challenges in terms of role ambiguity faced by SENCOs. Dyson and Gains (1995) assert that the coordinator's attempt to fulfil his or her purposes and to carry out a range of tasks and activities will only be successful insofar as he or she can manage the complex context in which they operate. To the extent that this context is characterised by the political issues regarding the control and direction of resources – a context in which people have different beliefs and values and where power is distributed unequally – it is suggested that the role of coordinator itself can be seen as 'unavoidably political in character'.

Certainly since the advent of the *Code of Practice for the Identification and Assessment of Special Educational Needs* (DFE 1994) there has been an increasing importance placed on the leadership role of the SENCO in terms of whole-school policy. Dyson and Gains argued that, as special needs provision is increasingly reconstructed in ways that are integral to the provision for all children, so the management of special needs becomes increasingly integrated into the overall management of the school. Our experience tends to indicate that the success of this evident good practice is inconsistent. In a study carried out into the role of the SENCO (Szwed 1997) the isolation factor was a strong feature that emerged from the data. Listening to the SENCOs, many found difficulties in working with other staff members at a time of 'initiative overload' and a 'payment by results philosophy'.

> People are set in their ways, they are reluctant to take on responsibility for children's special needs but I am slowly changing that by working alongside them. (High school SENCO)

The main pointers for success in the role (as indicated by the teachers in this small-scale study) were seen as a positive, supportive staff used to professional development, good support and encouragement from the head teacher and governors, and good communication with external agencies and parents. All of the teachers stressed the importance of management skills in developing their role.

The SENCO as teacher and manager

45

> I realised that many of the things I had been doing were unassertive and that I was not managing people well. I do not like to put pressure on people and so I was taking on too much unnecessary responsibility.   (Primary school SENCO)

In summary therefore, it is increasingly evident that the management role of the SENCO is crucial in the light of recent developments and, in particular, where there has been:

- an increase in the significance attached to the role resulting from the Code of Practice;
- an increased complexity of the role in practice;
- an increased importance of partnership between parents, schools and other agencies;
- increased importance of interpersonal skills in implementing change;
- increased potential for conflict and strain in the role in practice.

Part Two of this book considers the important area of communication, including issues relating to the monitoring and evaluation role such as giving and receiving feedback. The area of presentation skills is also included as this is a key area in relation to the professional development role of the SENCO.

Chapter 5

Managing pupil behaviour

In this part of the book we emphasise the significance of management and coordination skills within the area of coordination of special educational needs. In considering managing people, we also include a brief discussion relating to the management of pupil behaviour.

This is an area which is receiving a great deal of attention in the current political climate of social inclusion. All schools are now required to nominate a behaviour coordinator (who may or may not be the SENCO) and many schools and local authorities are promoting whole-school policies such as Assertive Discipline and Framework for Intervention. It is clear that the SENCO has a central role within this area and this chapter has been written to assist SENCOs to work in partnership with teachers, pupils, parents and associated professionals in order to analyse 'problem behaviour' from different perspectives and collaborate in devising effective interventions. It is also intended to assist the SENCO in advising colleagues, pupils and parents about strategies which can be used to prevent and manage problem behaviours.

Problem behaviour can be defined in many different ways. To some, the term conjures up images of pupils running riot. Others might be much more concerned about:

> a catalogue of comparatively minor misdemeanours which, whilst not immediately challenging the authority of teachers, demand the expenditure of inordinate amounts of teacher time and energy.
>
> (Charlton and David 1996, p. 7)

Some people relate problem behaviour directly to a 'disturbance' *within the child*, while others link it with the influence of factors *within the curriculum* (e.g. levels of literacy demanded in certain lessons), or the *learning environment* (e.g. amount and type of feedback given to pupils).

Galloway (1985) suggested that behaviour is problematic only when it becomes troublesome to someone. In other words a particular behaviour could be considered to be acceptable to one person (e.g. one teacher), while another person would consider it to be problematic. This can be potentially confusing for many children, hence the need for some (whole-school) agreement concerning standards of acceptable behaviour, methods of promoting such behaviour and ways of responding to infractions.

Defining 'problem behaviour'

Activity 5.1 (see p. 119)
Perceptions of 'problem behaviour'

The causes of problem behaviour

Beliefs about the causes of problem behaviours can have an important influence upon definitions. Some research (e.g. Croll and Moses 1985) reveals a tendency for teachers to attribute the causes of many problem behaviours to poor home conditions, or disturbing factors within the child. However, as Charlton and David (1996, p. 3) point out, there is a good deal of evidence to show that factors within schools affect their pupils' behaviour. These studies draw attention to the fact that schools with very similar catchment areas have markedly different incidences of problem behaviours. This leads Charlton and David to suggest that:

> What schools offer, and how they offer it, helps determine whether pupils respond in desirable or undesirable ways, and the reasons for pupils' misbehaviour may have as much (if not more) to do with experiences at school as those they encounter in the home, or with aspects of their personality. (p. 3)

More enlightened teachers will be aware of the range of causal factors, including the influences which the curriculum and their own behaviour can have upon the behaviour of their pupils. However, teachers must be wary of conceptualising problem behaviour solely on the basis of their own beliefs and understandings. Others (e.g. pupils, parents and associated professionals) will have a different perspective upon problem behaviours which can influence understandings and definitions. As Tisdall and Dawson (1994) suggest:

> there is a growing body of evidence which shows that, under the right conditions, pupils can provide useful insights into important matters which affect their learning. (p. 180)

Cooper (1996) draws particular attention to the valuable contribution which children who attract the 'emotional and behavioural difficulties' (EBD) label can make to our understanding of the conditions which affect behaviour:

> Many children who attract the EBD label often experience a wide range of difficulties of a social and personal nature, particularly in their family circumstances [Cooper 1993]. These difficulties make them especially vulnerable and sensitive to adverse aspects of their school environments. Children with EBD simply react more graphically than the majority of their peers to environmental circumstances that are experienced as negative by all pupils. They can, therefore, be seen as markers for such negative environmental circumstances. These circumstances need to be brought to light because they contribute to the development and maintenance of pupil deviance in schools. (p. 199)

Jones and Quah (1996) illustrate further the particular perceptions which pupils can have upon problem behaviours, through a discussion of the case of Gavin, an 11-year-old pupil who has a mixture of positive and negative learning experiences. Gavin's comments about the conditions which affect his social and academic learning reveal that he experiences success when he:

- feels able to ask for clarification about tasks and activities;
- is encouraged to find solutions to his own problems;
- is listened to with interest;
- is given positive rewards (verbal and non-verbal) for effort, achievement and acceptable behaviour;
- is allowed to seek support from other pupils, as well as seeking the advice of the teacher;
- receives explanations about undesirable behaviours.

In contrast, certain conditions seem to act as barriers to learning and cause Gavin to display what are deemed to be inappropriate behaviours. Under such conditions Gavin states that he is often:

- called names;
- scolded for doing things wrong;
- blamed for things he didn't do;
- labelled 'troublemaker' because of a genuine lack of understanding of task requirements;
- taught by impersonal or uncaring teachers.

Parents and other professionals can also make positive contributions to the understanding of problem behaviours. Jones and Lock (1993, p. 167) draw attention to research which shows that when confronted with problem behaviours some teachers and parents readily 'blame the other side' (Galloway 1985, p. 60). Jones and Lock go on to claim that:

> the development of a shared responsibility towards behaviour problems will allow for a deeper understanding of the whole range of factors which are relevant to a particular behaviour and subsequent responses to it. (p. 168)

The assessment of problem behaviours

Gross (1993) suggests that teachers often have a narrow view when it comes to assessing behaviour problems:

> There is a natural wish in many teachers to see assessment of behaviour difficulties in terms of discovering the deep seated causes of the child's failure to conform to behaviour expectations; usually the causes are seen as rooted in the home. (p. 95)

The adoption of such a narrow and negative approach is unhelpful and potentially hides a number of factors that have a significant influence upon pupil behaviour.

The most appropriate forms of assessment and provision will be those which take adequate account of the range of factors which influence pupil behaviour. To concentrate on any one, just because it is in fashion, could risk missing the heart of what causes a particular behaviour to become problematic.

The need for a comprehensive form of assessment, which takes account of behaviours in relation to the situations in which they occur, is also stressed in the *Code of Practice on the Identification and Assessment of Special Educational Needs* (DFE 1994). This Code of Practice also emphasises that *all* teachers have a central role in the assessment of behaviour problems. In discussing roles and responsibilities (para. 2:73) the Code states:

The child's teacher or tutor will:

- gather information about the child and make an initial assessment of the child's special educational needs;
- provide special help within the normal curriculum framework, exploring ways in which increased differentiation of classroom work might better meet the needs of the individual child;
- monitor and review the child's progress.

Para. 2:74 outlines the SENCO's role in relation to that of the class or subject teacher. It states that the SENCO will:

- ensure that the child is included in the school's SEN register;
- help the child's teacher or tutor to gather information and assess the child's needs;
- advise and support as necessary those who will teach the child.

The requirement for the child's teacher or tutor to collect and record a wide range of information is emphasised in para. 2:75. The information should come from the school, the parent, the child and other sources.

Problem behaviours can be assessed in a number of different ways. In the 'comparative' approach, a discussion of which follows, the main emphasis is upon 'comparing' a child's behaviour with that of peers.

The comparative approach

The main theme of this approach is a comparison of the quantity and/or qualities of a particular child's behaviour (or that of a group of children), with that of peers. Comparative methods are often used during the early stages of an assessment procedure, either for purposes of identification, or to clarify the extent or nature of a particular problem behaviour.

For example, in order to determine whether a child is deemed to have 'emotional and behavioural difficulties' the Code of Practice (DFE 1994) states that teachers and other professionals should determine whether:

- there is significant discrepancy between, on the one hand, the child's cognitive ability (and expectations thereof) and academic performance;
- the child is unusually withdrawn, lacks confidence and is unable to form purposeful and lasting relationships with peers and adults;
- there is evidence of severely impaired social interaction and communication, or a significantly restricted repertoire of activities, interests and imaginative development;
- the child attends school regularly;
- there is clear, recorded evidence of obsessional eating habits;
- there is clear, recorded evidence of any substance or alcohol misuse;

- the child displays unpredictable, bizarre, obsessive, violent or severely disruptive behaviour;
- the child has participated in or has been subject to bullying at school, or has been subject to neglect and/or abuse at home; and/or has faced major difficulties at home;
- there is any suggestion that the child may have a significant mental or physical health problem.

In answering many of the above questions (e.g. in order to determine whether a child is unusually withdrawn) a teacher, or associated professional, will have to make some form of *comparison* with other pupils.

Similarly, the following characteristics (see Cooper and Ideus 1996, p. 2), which are often used to draw attention to children who might have attention deficit hyperactivity disorder (ADHD), provide another clear example of the 'comparative' model of assessment.

Inattention

- Children with ADHD differ from their peers in the degree to which they appear to be able to sustain attention in tasks and play activities.
- They appear to be more easily distracted from tasks and play activities than their peers.
- They will also display extreme difficulties in starting and finishing schoolwork and other activities.
- They show a greater tendency than their peers to be inattentive and appear to ignore or find it impossible to follow instructions.
- They may also appear to be unusually disorganised and forgetful for their age.

Hyperactivity

- Their hyperactivity will manifest itself in unusually high levels of fidgeting, and unauthorised movement in the classroom situation or other situations where it is deemed inappropriate to roam freely.
- They will also show a greater tendency than their peers to want to run around and be 'on the go'.
- They are often noisy and over talkative, when compared with their peers.

Impulsivity

- Their impulsivity manifests itself in an over tendency to interrupt others, to butt into conversations, to have difficulty in waiting for their turn to participate in games or answer questions in class.

The presence of a combination of these characteristics would signal the need for a more in-depth assessment (see Cooper and Ideus 1996, for further details).

'Comparative' forms of assessment can help teachers, parents and other professionals characterise behaviours, to judge their severity against certain norms and to direct attention to the types of behaviour which are problematic. However, they are unlikely to provide sufficiently detailed information for the purposes of planning appropriate responses to, or the prevention of, behaviour problems. Having served to focus attention on particular behaviours, they will need to be followed up by more detailed forms of assessment, which examine factors 'within the learner', 'the curriculum' and 'the learning environment'. Different forms of assessment which fall under these headings are considered in the following sections of this chapter.

Assessing factors within the learner

The assessments which are undertaken to diagnose causal factors 'within the learner' vary from child to child according to their particular needs and may include an examination of factors such as hearing, vision, sensory processing, temperament, biochemical conditions and affective factors (self-concept and locus of control). While the latter will be influenced by factors within the wider learning environment, they will be considered initially within this section.

Basically, under this approach a diagnosis is made of certain factors within the learner which appear to be contributing towards a problem behaviour. This is then followed by some kind of prescribed action, designed to improve conditions for learning and hence reduce the occurrence, or magnitude of that behaviour.

Jones (1992) and Jones and Charlton (1996) discuss factors within the learner which can contribute towards behaviour problems. The most obvious, and sometimes overlooked, factors are the quality of hearing and vision. If problems of hearing and vision are not detected a pupil is likely to encounter considerable difficulties in learning. This in turn can lead to considerable frustration which could cause some pupils to behave in socially unacceptable ways. Some might retreat into withdrawn behaviours, while others might seek attention through more active, aggressive, means.

Other less obvious, sensory processing factors can influence learning and behaviour outcomes (see Tyler 1990). For example a child with specific learning difficulties in the auditory area (e.g. poor level of hearing and/or difficulties in discriminating between sounds), but strengths in the visual and kinaesthetic channels, will experience considerable difficulties in learning when faced with a teacher who relies almost wholly on verbal explanations, without any supportive visual or manipulative resources. The following statement, written by a student during initial training, indicates that teachers can better respond to the needs of all learners in a class if they adopt a multi-sensory approach to teaching and learning:

> the more media available to the teacher the more chances students have to fully comprehend the subject. The teacher employs a variety of media such as verbal symbols (textbooks), visual symbols (charts), photos, recordings, films, exhibits, field trips, demonstrations, drama, contrived and direct purposeful experiences, to differentially cater to the stronger sense of the students. (Jones and Charlton 1996, p. 130)

It is interesting to note that many teachers, and associated professionals, predominantly rely upon the auditory mode (spoken instructions) when they attempt to manage problem behaviours. To put it simply, pupils are most often 'told about' a behaviour, rather than being 'shown' what to do. Hence the common use of the term '*told* off'.

Other factors, 'within the learner', such as diet and genetic make-up, can have a direct effect upon behaviour. For example, it has been suggested that particular types of temperament may predispose young children to later maladjustment (Thomas and Chess 1977). Such predispositions include under- and over-activity, tendency to withdrawal and irregularity of sleeping. Charlton and George (1993, p. 22–31) produce a good account of such factors and the effects which they can have upon learning and behaviour.

Ideus (1991) draws attention to the fact that attention deficit hyperactivity disorder (ADHD) has its source 'within the learner':

> ADHD is understood as a genetically inherited, biologically based disorder in which dysregulation of certain brain chemicals causes affected individuals to have problems with paying attention, controlling impulsivity and regulating levels of motor activity.
>
> (p. 178)

However, as Crew and Woodcock (1996) point out, the successful management of ADHD must take into account a range of factors, not all of which reside 'within the learner'.

However, while the above factors are important and should be taken into account, few behaviour problems will have causes which are solely related to factors 'within the learner'. For this reason 'within learner factors' must be considered alongside other causal factors, within 'the curriculum' and 'the learning environment'.

Assessing factors within the curriculum

A number of researchers have claimed that an inappropriate curriculum is a major source of problem behaviours (e.g. Charlton 1986, Reynolds 1984). Charlton comments that those:

> who are disinterested in, or disenchanted with the educational programmes schools offer to them, may well direct their interest and energies away from school tasks towards a variety of maladaptive behaviours (e.g. non-involvement in academic work, truancy, abuse towards teachers) which facilitate an excitement and involvement unavailable elsewhere in school.   (p. 70)

This was clearly illustrated in the study conducted by staff at the Centre for Special Educational Needs (University College Worcester) and staff at the Centre for Behaviour Studies (Cheltenham and Gloucester College of Higher Education) concerning the relationship between the curriculum and pupil exclusion (QCA 1998). A Head of Year (referring to a Year 9 pupil) made the following comments:

> In many areas he's still right at the bottom of the performance league. Even though he tried very hard, there was virtually no success. In some areas, like sport, or being able to fight, he could be as good, if not better, than other lads in his year.

For some children, the planned curriculum, without modification, moves too fast, is at too difficult a level and/or is lacking in purpose.

Others become frustrated because they are constantly revising work which is already familiar to them and which moves at too slow a pace. This is true for both academic and social learning and both aspects should be considered when examining causal factors within the 'curriculum'.

Teachers are often alerted to problems in the curriculum through the 'products' of pupil learning (e.g. incorrect verbal or written responses, uncoordinated motor actions, inappropriate behaviours). Such responses can signal that the level, or pace, of the curriculum is inappropriate for a particular child. The following comments from a pupil and a parent further emphasise the need to ensure that work is at an appropriately challenging level:

'It ain't hard and it 'aint easy, just about right [art]. (Year 9 pupil)

'He obviously found it interesting [maths]. I think it was mind boggling enough to keep his attention a bit longer than other subjects did. He likes a good challenge. (Parent of a Year 8 pupil)

The process of 'task' analysis can be used to examine whether the various stages of learning (academic or social) are achievable, yet challenging, for a particular pupil. Briefly this involves the following steps:

- a detailed description of the various sub-stages within a task;
- the child's current level of performance is established, together with an analysis of the conditions under which he or she can do it and the level of success achieved;
- a series of incremental learning objectives are planned, each one building upon the other.

An example, from the teaching of mathematics, is provided by Haylock (1991, p. 61):

> calculate, by an informal adding-on process, the time interval from one digital time to another

> tell the time, to nearest five minutes from a dial clock, or watch, giving the answer in the form 3.40 a.m.

> time activities or events, in seconds using the second counter of a digital watch, starting from zero, or a simple stop clock or stop watch

Activities may then be provided to help the child to achieve each of the objectives and thus reach the predetermined goal. 'Task analysis' can also be used to set targets for the teaching of certain social behaviours.

The 'length' of tasks also has an important influence upon academic and social behaviour. A number of respondents in the aforementioned research (Haylock 1991) drew attention to the fact that many of the pupils in the sample had a short attention span. In their opinion those pupils were not able to cope with lengthy tasks and encountered particular difficulties during double lessons. Additionally, some considered that pupils were overburdened with the cumulative amount of work which was required of them. For other, more able pupils, the amount of work was insufficient or unchallenging.

While many teachers might be alerted to possible causes of problem behaviours through an analysis of the 'products' of children's learning they might overlook difficulties which children encounter with the 'processes' of learning. For many years there has been a tendency to task analyse the curriculum on the basis of 'products' of learning, to the detriment of an accompanying analysis of the processes by which children learn.

Smith (1994), in discussing the relative complexity of different learning processes, claims that children will:

- find it more difficult to reason abstractly than with the use of concrete materials; it will be harder for them to add abstract numerals than to perform similar calculations with blocks, or real coins;
- sometimes be unable to respond through spoken language, while they can do so through non-verbal means;
- encounter greater difficulties in expressing what they know, rather than dealing with the same material receptively.

Learning style also has an important influence upon behaviour. If the child is expected to perform tasks which are not compatible with their learning style, they will become frustrated, bored and will sometimes resort to 'withdrawn' or 'aggressive' behaviours. For example, some pupils with specific learning difficulties might perform much better if they were allowed to record their thoughts in the form of 'mind maps' (similar to topic webs), rather than in continuous prose. Those whose learning is 'blocked' by an overemphasis on pen and paper activities, may be pleasantly surprised to find that new technology (e.g. spell-masters and voice recognition technology) can help them to process learning in new and exciting ways, thus reducing their frustration and thereby preventing the occurrence of inappropriate behaviours.

Learning difficulties and behaviour problems can also be caused by a 'perceived lack of purpose'. Writers of a UNESCO study pack (1993) claim that children who are not getting on with their work in class almost always seem to lack understanding as to the purpose of what they have been asked to do. When children are asked why they are doing something, many will say that they are doing it because their teacher told them to. Very rarely do they relate it to any purpose which is personal to them. This is unfortunate because, as the aforementioned writers suggest:

> Learning is about finding personal meanings from experience. It requires us to understand what we are about and relate this to our existing knowledge and previous experience. Consequently, if we are unclear about the purpose of an activity, learning is less likely. Effective teachers stress meaning in their work. They find ways of helping their pupils understand the purposes of particular tasks, the reasons why they have been set, how they are to be carried out and by when. (UNESCO 1993)

Additionally, if pupils do not understand why they are doing a particular task, they will not have any control over it. At best, they will need to refer constantly back to the teacher for clarification and help.

As mentioned earlier, the factors which have been discussed above apply equally to the learning of social behaviour. Pupils will respond poorly to the social curriculum if it is not pitched at an appropriately challenging level, if it is seen to lack purpose to their own lives, or if it is presented to them in an abstract way.

Of even greater concern, to many teachers, associated professionals and parents, is the perceived *lack* of an adequate personal and social curriculum in schools. Some suggest that pupils should be entitled, at a minimum, to a personal and social education which helps to develop:

- self-awareness and self-esteem;
- listening and communication skills;
- interpersonal skills (including how to make and keep friends, work in teams, trust peers and adults);
- negotiation skills;
- acceptance of boundaries, anger management and conflict resolution;
- an understanding of how society works;
- means of coping with authority.

The absence of direct, or permeated, teaching of some of these topics within schools and homes, may cause some pupils to encounter unnecessary difficulties. For this reason, their absence should be viewed as a potential causal factor to certain problem behaviours. It is hoped that the introduction of citizenship education into our schools may go some way to meeting these needs.

Assessing factors 'within the learning environment'

While physical aspects of the 'learning environment' (such as the quality and quantity of resources) are the most visible factors which can influence pupil behaviour, they are not necessarily the most important (Jones and Charlton 1996). Other, less visible features, can easily be overlooked. A number of researchers (e.g. Mortimore *et al.* 1988, Bennett 1991, Cooper 1996) have drawn attention to certain factors which can precipitate and maintain difficulties in learning, some of which are noted below (Jones and Charlton 1996, pp. 24–6):

- poor specification of the learning task;
- ineffective time management, thus reducing the amount of time available for teaching;
- few opportunities to review, revise and reinforce learning;
- the work having an image inappropriate to the pupil's chronological age;
- lack of purpose in learning activities;
- inappropriate grouping activities;
- absence of teaching approaches which encourage independent learning, poor social skills, thus leading to inappropriate behaviours in certain situations;
- inconsistency among teachers;
- lack of a clear theme in lessons;
- poor record keeping;
- lack of peer support.

Charlton (1992) claims that affective factors, such as the beliefs pupils hold about themselves as learners (e.g. their 'self-concept') are crucial in determining academic and social learning outcomes. As Lambley (1993) describes:

> The self-concept is fashioned by the individual's interpretation of feedback on his or her performances from significant others such as parents, peers and teachers. Feedback plays a crucial role for the child in defining his or her self-perception of ability. If the performance is satisfactory, future tasks are likely to be approached with confidence.

Lambley draws attention to the positive outcomes which can accrue when the child receives good feedback. Alternatively, when good feedback is not forthcoming problems can arise, as illustrated in one teacher's comments:

> For a very long time he'd been told he wasn't good at things and he shielded that by being boisterous and aggressive at times. An aggressive facade, and underneath it, there's someone saying can't someone help me. They can't express it in normal ways.
>
> (Teacher of a Year 9 pupil)

Other affective factors (e.g. 'locus of control') will determine the extent to which pupils believe they are in control of their academic and social learning (see also Chapter 3).

Another key factor 'within the learning environment' which can influence academic and social learning is the nature of teacher–pupil relationships. The aforementioned research revealed that learning outcomes were related to certain characteristics of teacher–pupil relationships, such as the extent to which pupils felt 'listened to', 'liked', and 'trusted'.

It was considered that relaxed, comfortable and purposeful relationships, in which teachers were perceived to be tuned in to pupils' interests were most effective for pupils with emotional and behavioural difficulties, while autocratic and confrontational relationships tended to demotivate them. Some pupils were disaffected because they felt they were labelled, according to the reputation of relatives who currently attend, or previously attended, the school.

Evidence of the positive influence which teacher behaviour can have upon pupil behaviour was found in research conducted by Charlton *et al.* (1996).

In contrast to the positive influences, referred to in Charlton *et al.*'s study, Reynolds (1984) draws attention to a range of negative factors which are associated with high-vandalism and high disaffection:

- a coercive regime where control is more concerned with physically punishing, rather than seeking the root cause of, deviant behaviour, where many rules prevailed and were inflexibly enforced;
- relationships between teachers and pupils being marked by friction;
- the head teacher and staff apportioning the blame for school problems upon each other;
- a high turnover of staff;
- a paucity of pupil involvement in running the school;

- classroom management practices which include public ridicule of miscreants and the administration of class punishment for individual rule breaking;
- an unwillingness to welcome parents into the school;
- an iniquitous investment of staff expertise, time, energy and other resources into 'A' streams and a consequent low, or inferior, investment into other classes;
- negative staff perceptions of pupils who were seen as irredeemable and as having irremediable problems, stemming from apparent deficiencies in primary socialisation.

Pupil behaviour will also be influenced by the dynamics of groups and individual friendships. In some cases the peer group will exert a strong influence on a pupil which will lead to undesirable behaviour, while for others it will offer a positive, mediating effect which will prevent, or dampen down the occurrence of a particular behaviour. For this reason, pupil grouping within classrooms should be examined carefully. Despite considerable literature on the perceived benefits which can accrue from small groupwork, the pupils who were the subjects of the research into 'exclusion' appeared to perform better when they were working alone. This was attributed to the belief that the majority of pupils either distracted, or were distracted by, peers, or lacked the social skills with which to effectively participate in cooperative learning tasks.

Other pupils are emotionally upset by the fact that they do not feel accepted by their peers. In some cases this can lead to withdrawn behaviour which will militate against learning. Tisdall and Dawson's (1994) research draws attention to the sense of isolation which many pupils experience. As one pupil said:

> It's sort of like an outsider coming in [to the group] and, like, it's quite hard to get accepted.

In some cases the emotional pressures which are inflicted upon a particular child will create a total block to learning.

Activity 5.2 (see pp. 120–122)
Factors associated with problem behaviour

Summary

Problem behaviours can be caused by a whole range of factors, some of which reside 'within the learner', while others are associated with 'the curriculum' or the 'learning environment'. A failure to consider adequately any one of these groups of factors is to risk overlooking the very heart of what might affect academic and/or social learning for a particular pupil. While many of these factors will be 'visible' to teachers, some will be hidden from their view.

There will be significant pupils and parents who will be better placed to see the importance of those 'hidden' factors. It is crucial that an analysis of factors which appear to be associated with a particular problem behaviour should be conducted by teachers and associated professionals in partnership with pupils and their parents or carers. It is only when all these views are taken into account that we can develop a whole child perspective and develop effective strategies to promote positive behaviour.

Chapter 6

Communication skills – giving and receiving information

In a consideration of managing people, it is clear that a SENCO has to be able to manage and work in conjunction with a variety of people from varying backgrounds and varying experiences. These include pupils, parents, other teachers in the school, governors, learning support assistants (LSAs) and a wide range of professionals from a wide range of external agencies. In fact it could be argued that a SENCO is involved in a far greater range of communication situations than other subject coordinators. As noted in the SENCO Standards, the area of leading and managing staff is of great importance and it is evident that to do this well a SENCO requires good interpersonal and communication skills (TTA 1998).

Research undertaken by the University of Newcastle upon Tyne in 1995 on the introduction of the Code of Practice (reported in *The Senco Guide*, DfEE 1997a) suggested that three of the key challenges for a SENCO were:

- the management of time;
- liaison with colleagues, parents, external agencies and governors;
- developing the in-service training recommended by the Code.

To meet these challenges the SENCO needs to consider carefully the whole area of communication, trying to ensure that lines of communication are open, honest and clear to all parties. In this chapter we intend to examine some of the factors which contribute to effective communication.

Social psychology research shows that seven out of every ten minutes of our waking lives is spent in communication. It has been suggested that this figure is even higher in our working lives, where an average of 78 per cent of all activity is devoted to communication. Yet few managers realise how much time is spent in conversation and many actually feel that it interferes with the 'real' job.

Communication is a complex process requiring many different skills. In day to day life we communicate:

with various *people*
in various *situations*
with different *purposes*
using different *methods*.

Most people are able to move swiftly between different situations, adapting their skills to suit the situation without even giving it much conscious thought. But it is possible to become an even more effective communicator and, importantly, to avoid some of the many pitfalls.

> **Activity 6.1 (see pp. 122–123)**
> **Who does a SENCO communicate with?**

A list generated by a group of SENCOs who carried out Activity 6.1 demonstrates the extensive communication they are involved in: it included, teachers, pupils, parents, governors, LSAs, inspectors, colleagues from other schools, as well as all the external agencies and staff that a SENCO needs to negotiate with.

Types of interaction

This chapter focuses on 'face to face' communication within the school and work environment. This includes verbal and non-verbal aspects of communication. There follow four different types of interaction, each of which has a different purpose.

Giving information

This is one of the simplest forms of communication. The emphasis is on sending a message and looking for feedback to test whether it is being received accurately.

> Examples of this kind of communication include giving instructions, feedback, reporting back, presentations and lectures. The emphasis is on the need to be clear and to pick up feedback on how the message is being received.

Receiving information

In this type of communication the main object is to gain information.

> Examples of this kind of communication are meetings with parents, and listening to pupils. The main skills in gaining information are questioning, listening and checking out. The draft revised Code of Practice (DfEE 2000) places a great deal of emphasis on gaining pupils' views and this is an area in which good practice is inconsistent.

Further very helpful information on listening to pupils will be found in the article 'Helping children to find a voice' by Lewis (1996) (see Bibliography).

Solving problems

In this situation the answer is not known to either party in advance of the conversation. The aim is to exchange information to create a picture which is helpful to both parties but beyond the power of either to create single-handedly. It is a collaborative exercise requiring both parties to work together with a degree of mutual trust.

> Examples of this kind of communication are review and planning meetings between SENCOs, class/subject teachers, parents, pupils and associated professionals.

Resolving conflict

This last category is the most complex and potentially time-consuming. It is also a communicative situation in which the answer is not known beforehand. However, in this case the different parties usually have objectives which are at odds with each other.

> An example of this kind of communication could be a meeting between a SENCO and a class/subject teacher, who have different views about the support requirements of a particular pupil.

The model of communication shown in Figure 6.1 helps to focus attention on the skills involved and some of the problems which might be encountered.

A model of communication

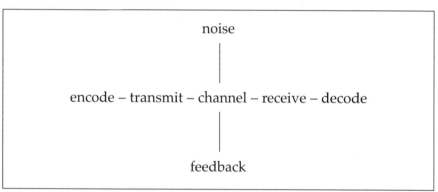

Figure 6.1 Model of communication

As the model shows, messages are encoded and transmitted. They are received and decoded. There are many stages in this process which can go wrong.

(a) There can be problems **at source**. These can occur when ideas are not clearly formulated, through the use of technical words or jargon, or when vocabulary is used inappropriately. It is important to think carefully about using terms such as SATs, OFSTED, etc., to parents, who may not be familiar with them.
(b) There can be problems with the **channel of communication**. The receiver may be too busy or preoccupied to give their attention to the message. The situation may be inappropriate for the communication. There may be too much 'noise' for good communication (e.g. too many things going on at the time). Sometimes it is simply a matter of bad timing.
(c) Even when a message is transmitted accurately and there is a good channel of communication, it does not necessarily mean that it will be received. **The message may not be heard**, for many reasons:
  – the wishes and feelings of the listener: people hear what they want to hear and respond differently on different days;
  – the background and experience of the listener: people try to make sense of the world and will interpret messages so that they make sense to them (think of the range of interpretations of a simple message in the chinese whispers game);

– the beliefs and attitudes of the listener: people have a tendency to take in information which fits in with their expectations and to ignore information which is contrary to them; first impressions are important as they help to define our expectations.

It is important that we are aware of the difficulties that may arise and consider ways of eliminating some of these difficulties.

Listening is one of the most important aspects of communication. This involves trying to make sense of what the other person is really saying.

Another crucial aspect of effective communication is **feedback**. This provides the speaker with an opportunity to add to, clarify and change their message. The process of communication is mutual and circular. A good communicator is a person who is responsive to feedback (verbal and non-verbal) and alters their message in the light of it. Feedback will be examined more fully in Chapter 7.

In summary, *a good communicator must*:

- have good timing
- gain attention
- give clear messages
- look for feedback
- listen well
- adapt what they say in the light of feedback
- give good feedback.

Communication styles

When someone comes to you with a problem you have many options. On the one hand you can tell them exactly what to do and how to do it. On the other hand you can leave the problem firmly with them. There is a whole range of communication styles in between these extremes (Figure 6.2).

A range of communication styles

Refusing to get involved at all

Passive listening

Active listening

Interpreting

Diagnosing

Adding new information

Identifying the options

Recommending what to do

Telling what to do

Telling what to do and how to do it

Figure 6.2 Range of communication styles

There is considerable overlap between these aspects and in any one interaction you can find yourself moving between states depending on the kind of problems which arise. It is important to find out what the person bringing the problem wants to get out of their discussion with you. Mismatches in expectations can cause problems. It is also important not to go beyond the limitations of your expertise. As a SENCO you have access to a range of professional expertise which may be more appropriate to draw from.

Listening skills

Most people believe that they are good listeners. It can come as quite a shock to find that listening is very difficult and that most of us do not listen effectively. There is a tendency to think that the person making the biggest contribution in a social situation is the one doing most of the talking. In fact the person who does most of the listening can often have the most significant effect on a group. It is often a revelation to realise the creative and powerful effect that good listening can have.

Examples of poor listening abound. On TV it is rare for someone being interviewed to listen to what they are being asked. The temptation is to be eager and put across our own point of view. People involved in arguments can be so busy trying to get their view across that they fail to realise what common ground they have.

Difficulties in listening

People listen least when they are most anxious to speak.

> A common example of this is during staff meetings. When people approach a point at which they are eager to say something, they are likely to block out what other people are saying in order to rehearse what they want to say. The best chance of being listened to is to let the other person speak first.

People stop listening when they think they know what the other person is going to say.

> In fact, this is the very point at which they probably need to listen more carefully.

People find it hard to listen when their emotions are upset or the atmosphere is tense.

> This can account for many of the misunderstandings which can arise between people. People often hear words, but cannot 'take them in'. When we are upset or annoyed we need to listen carefully to what is being said in order to overcome the communication difficulties.

People stop listening when they pick up inaccuracies in some unimportant detail.

> They then wait to feed this back rather than listening to the essential message.

People stop listening when one person speaks for too long.

> The longer a person speaks the harder it becomes for someone to concentrate on what is being said.

People stop listening when they feel that the speaker is hiding their true feelings behind the words they use. Remember, your body language can indicate your true feelings.

People stop listening if a discussion turns into an argument. They then become more interested in winning than in listening.

People tend to evaluate what is being said according to their evaluation of the speaker as a person. If someone has low credibility, people are less likely to give credence to what they have to say, irrespective of the quality of what they are saying. (It is helpful to note that the draft Code of Practice (DfEE 2000) aims to raise the status of the SENCO.)

[?] *Activity 6.2 (see p. 123)*
'Out talking your partner'

[?] *Activity 6.3 (see p. 123)*
'Brick-walling'

Active listening

Good listening requires a considerable amount of energy and effort. It is an active rather than a passive activity. The aims of active listening are:

– to try to understand and accept the situation from the other person's point of view;
– to help the other person to talk about the situation as they see it;
– to help them to clarify their own feelings;
– to help them to make progress in solving their own problem.

Table 6.1 provides examples of what can help, and hinder, listening.

Non-verbal communication

Another important part of the communication process is non-verbal communication. This has many functions in enhancing communication. It helps to:

– communicate attitudes and emotions;
– convey information about self;
– support verbal communication (e.g. gaining attention, adding emphasis).

Aspects of non-verbal communication

• **facial expression** – we communicate about our emotional state through our facial expression. The eyebrows and mouth carry a lot

Table 6.1 What helps and hinders listening

Listening In terms of	What helps	What hinders
Responses – verbal	good attention reflecting open-ended questions accepting silence	poor attention me too put down if I were you interrupting
Responses – non-verbal	open posture comfortable distance non-threatening gaze	closed posture inappropriate distance looking bored and yawning
Feelings	calm at ease receptive not distracted	aroused or angry emotional preoccupied
The setting	calm enough time	distractions discomfort pressure of time

of information. There is a high level of agreement between people about what different expressions indicate;

- **gaze** – looking at other people in (the area of) the face is a way of collecting information about how a message is being received. It is also a way of synchronising communication. We use signals to indicate when one person has nearly finished and is waiting for the other to come in (e.g. looking at the other person directly and raising the eyebrows);
- **gestures** – when a person speaks they invariably move their hands, body and head continuously. This can give illustration, provide emphasis, act as reinforcement, reflect emotional states;
- **posture** – people show their feelings by their posture. Tallness tends to signal dominance. If people want to be assertive they will sit straight and upright. Positive feelings are indicated by leaning forward, touching, getting close, orienting oneself to the other person. The opposite of this is leaning away, turning away, breaking eye contact, leaving as soon as possible after an encounter. A signal of support and friendship is postural echo where one person unconsciously echoes the posture of another;
- **contact** – bodily contact in our culture is controlled by strict rules. The handshake is an important first point of contact and can influence first impressions;
- **use of space** – physical proximity and orientation. It is interesting to observe people's use of space. You can pick up how people are getting on by their physical proximity and orientation. People who

are negotiating or arguing will often sit opposite each other. People wanting to cooperate will sit next to each or at a 90 degree angle. If they are standing at a greater angle they are probably hoping to be rescued!
- **physical appearance** – people form impressions of others on the basis of what they look like. Attractive people are rated highly on a number of other unrelated criteria (e.g. more intelligent, more honest).

 Activity 6.4 (see p. 124)
Giving attention

Many SENCOs have reported to us certain difficulties in communicating with parents/carers regarding allocation of support time, etc. It is helpful to try to remain aware of the challenges certain meetings, such as Annual Reviews can present, and focus on some of the approaches illustrated in Table 6.2.

It is also important to remember that we can all improve our communication skills. Activities 6.2–6.5 provide practical opportunities to try out some of the ideas discussed in this chapter.

 Activity 6.5 (see p. 124)
Giving feedback

Summary

It is evident that effective communication is a fundamental aspect of the SENCO's role. Developing good communication skills helps to ensure understanding, cooperation, team work and development and these are all key to the modern SENCO's role. As Gross (2000) suggests, the role of the SENCO needs to shift from 'paper processor to consultant on teaching and learning'. Therefore another key area to consider is that of giving positive and constructive feedback and it is to this that we turn in the next chapter.

Table 6.2 Skills required for good communication

Good communication requires certain skills, such as:

Paying attention

facing the other person;
adopting an open posture;
leaning towards each other;
keeping good eye contact;
giving appropriate facial
   expression;
nodding.

Paraphrasing

This involves restating what you have heard clearly and simply. It helps you to clarify in your own words what you think the speaker is saying and helps you to check this out with the speaker who can then correct any mis-understandings.

Clarifying and checking

For example: 'I'm not sure I've got this right. Who was there at the time?'

It is important to be able to admit confusion, ask for a restatement, check out your understanding.

Using open-ended questions

For example: 'Can you tell me more about that?', 'How did that make you feel?'

Specific questions

These can be useful to show interest in the detail of what is being said.

Echoing

Simply repeating back part of what they have said.

Being non-judgemental

This avoids the tendency for people to clam up. Non-verbal clues are also important here.

Asking for examples

This aids understanding of the other person's situation.

Use of feeling

For example: 'That sounds dreadful for you?' People are more likely to talk if they feel you are able to empathise as well as understand.

Reflecting feeling

For example: 'That must have made you very angry.'

Use of silence

This can be very effective.

Chapter 7

Communication skills – influencing others

In the past managers have been categorised as 'primarily concerned with *people*' or 'primarily concerned with *results*'. There is increasing recognition that the effective manager manages people so that both the organisation and the individuals involved feel the benefit. People who feel good about themselves produce good results. Not all professionals share the same philosophy or even focus on special educational needs and it has often been pointed out to us that some teachers are unwilling or unable to take on board their responsibilities in this area. As the SENCO moves more towards a consultative role it is clear that not all communication situations will be positive. In this chapter we examine improving motivation, giving feedback relating to performance, how we may become more effective in influencing others through improved negotiating skills, trying to resolve conflict situations, and how we can give and receive criticism effectively. There are several signs and reasons for lack of motivation (Table 7.1).

Table 7.1 Signs of and reasons for lack of motivation

Signs of a lack of motivation	Reasons for lack of motivation
absenteeism lateness non-participation sudden anger poor work	lack of recognition boredom lack of involvement criticism too much work to do/inadequate resources lack of development opportunities

Strategies to increase motivation

The following are essential approaches when seeking to improve motivation.

- The setting of clear goals and areas of responsibility.
- The provision of feedback about performance – which can be either 'positive' or 'criticism'.

> *Positive:* The norm is for people to give feedback about mistakes, but little or no feedback for good work. People need recognition and appreciation for their work – positive feedback encourages performance.

Criticism: It is important not to ignore unsatisfactory performance as this leads to increasingly poor performance. It has been estimated that 50 per cent of problems are due to lack of feedback. People tend to ignore problems rather than tackle them because they find giving negative feedback so uncomfortable. It is an issue which is often handled badly.

- Ensuring people are informed and involved.
- Valuing people as individuals.
- Giving responsibility and opportunities for achievement.

The provision of feedback

For *positive feedback* to be effective it needs to be:

- genuine;
- not a precursor to criticism;
- given for effort as well as achievement;
- immediate;
- frequent initially, then intermittent.

For *criticism* to be effective it needs to be:

- immediate, and for one thing at a time (it is tempting to let things mount up);
- factual (it may be necessary to check facts first);
- specific to the behaviour, not the person;
- to the point (not beating about the bush);
- non-judgemental;
- delivered calmly;
- delivered in a way that shows care about the individual.

It is important to distinguish between what people can't or won't do. People should not be criticised for what they cannot do. Table 7.2 provides suggestions for offering constructive criticism.

Giving feedback requires sensitivity to the feelings of others. Constructive feedback does not imply a situation where there are no difficulties but it is important to remember that as a SENCO you may be dealing with people who have low self-esteem or others (parents, pupils) who are not confident about their own ability or understanding of a situation.

 Activity 7.1 (see p. 125)
Giving appropriate feedback

Through the provision of positive feedback and constructive criticism people can attempt to 'influence' the professional practices (and other behaviours) of their colleagues, friends, relatives and peers. The following section invites you to examine the ways in which you, habitually, influence others.

Table 7.2 Offering constructive criticism

1	Headline	Use a headline to get to the point (e.g. 'David, I'd like to talk to you about the time of arriving in school.')
2	Checking out	Confirm the facts and listen to what the other person has to say about the problem (e.g. 'I've noticed that it's five to nine when you come in these days. Is there a problem at home or is anything else the matter?')
3	Effect of problem	If still appropriate, restate the problem behaviour clearly and describe the effect it has (e.g. 'When you come in at five to nine I am concerned that you are not well or there is something else the matter.)
4	Desired outcome	Describe what you would like to see happening and the positive effects (e.g. 'If you were in school before quarter to nine I would know you were alright and I would not worry.')
5	End on a positive note	For example: 'I'm glad I said something. I was getting worried about you. You have always been very punctual in the past. It was one of the things I first noticed about you.'

Influencing others

Influence can be: **overt** (e.g. from job title, number of people for whom you are responsible); **active** (e.g. your ability to influence, skills, knowledge).

Influence can be achieved through:

- ability, knowledge and skills;
- reputation and track record;
- ability to reward and deliver sanctions;
- having an overview;
- physical attributes and attractiveness;
- money;
- personal confidence;
- title/status.

Although you may be in a position of 'authority' as a SENCO and able to make decisions regarding others' futures, influence may be better achieved through effective listening and communication skills.

It is also important to consider how you appear to others and what personal communication strategies you use to achieve influence.

? *Activity 7.2 (see p. 125)*
Ways of influencing others

Three types of approach are suggested by commentators such as Back and Back (1982).

1. Push – The forceful approach. You already use this approach if you:

- let others know what you want and need;
- let others know what standards you expect;
- are comfortable instructing, directing and correcting others;
- are quick to praise and criticise;
- voice your own opinion frequently;
- like to bargain;
- find it easy to put pressure on others.

This approach will be useful to you if you:

- don't like talking about yourself;
- appear indecisive and submissive;
- cannot say no;
- avoid conflict;
- compromise too readily.

There are three elements to this approach:

(a) saying what you want and need;
(b) describing what you like and don't like;
(c) using the carrot and stick.

Assertive messages have three parts:

describe	– 'When you don't return my calls…'
disclose	– 'I get frustrated…'
predict	– 'I know you're busy, but if you phoned back it would save us both time.'

2. Pull – The participative approach. You already use this approach if you:

- ask people for opinions;
- notice and respond to other people's concerns;
- try to bring in people who are isolated;
- pay attention to views other than your own;
- actively supply others with information;
- are open with your thoughts and feelings.

This approach will be useful to you if you:

- always control or dominate;
- talk too much and do not let others have their say;
- listen poorly;
- are regarded as pushy.

There are three elements to this approach:

(a) involving others
(b) active listening
(c) disclosing.

3. Exit. You already use this approach if you:

- delay dealing with issues until you are prepared;
- allow other people time to prepare;
- stop discussion when you are overloaded;
- step back from the problem and analyse what is going on.

You will find this approach useful if you:

- have difficulty distancing yourself from situations;
- keep going when you need time to reflect;
- get involved in conflict;
- respond to personal attack by getting angry or upset.

So far in this chapter, we have examined ways in which people can communicate with and influence each other within reasonably straightforward contexts. However, there will be times when people have to communicate for the purpose of resolving conflict. We now examine ways in which communication skills can be used in more challenging situations.

Resolving conflict

The resolution of conflict situations requires skilled communication. The situation requires problem-solving skills but, in addition, the situation is likely to be highly charged with emotion. Both parties may behave aggressively and this creates a high level of risk. We are going to focus on one approach to resolving conflict – through negotiation.

In conflict situations, people:

- Do not listen. While one person is talking the other is thinking about what they are going to say next.
- Tend to become more entrenched in their views. The more they are forced to argue for a position the more committed they become.
- Tend to make early judgements about solutions.
- Focus on winning or getting their own way rather than looking for solutions to problems. People begin to feel that they cannot back down and worry about losing face.
- Become emotionally involved. They can become angry or defensive or upset.
- Make personal comments and judgements rather than being factual.

Suggestions for negotiating:

- Find a neutral and non-threatening setting (e.g. with a cup of coffee, sitting down, small talk).
- Maximise your information about the other person – their arguments, interests and feelings. Put yourself in their shoes. Think about their interests as well as your own. Behind the conflict you may have many interests in common. Spend time listening. Recognise their needs. Acknowledge what the other person says to you and reflect it back to see whether you have got it right. Acknowledge their feelings and concerns.

- Be honest about your point of view, explain the constraints under which you are working, acknowledge your own feelings and worries.
- Look for a range of options not just the one right answer. Discuss the range of options and possibilities. Generate a variety of possibilities before deciding what to do.
- Look for 'better for both' solutions. Ask the other person for their preference. Look for face-saver options.
- Remain calm and patient.
- Watch out for non-verbal signs, look for danger signs (e.g. raised voice, standing up, invasion of personal space, aggressive gestures, body posture) and work to diffuse them (low-voice, non-dominant posture, not touching).

Receiving negative feedback can leave a person feeling threatened, undervalued and disappointed. It is important to remember that people who feel vulnerable or lack self-confidence are more likely to offer negative feedback. It is always worth trying to ask why criticism has been offered and then to work out strategies for dealing with it.

Dealing assertively with criticism from others

Criticism

When we are criticised we may respond in a number of ways:

Apologetic	– 'I'm terribly sorry', 'I'm so sorry', 'I'm awfully sorry', and, maybe seeking forgiveness, 'Please forgive me'.
Defensive	'No, I did not', 'Not me, I couldn't help it', 'It's not my fault'.
Attacking	– 'How dare you blame me!' Who do you think you are? 'Don't come to me with your problems.'
Say nothing	– Which may be taken as meaning we accept the criticism.

Underneath our responses may be some of the thoughts shown in Table 7.3.

Table 7.3 Responses to criticism

A fear of being disliked	– for me to be O.K. it is absolutely essential that I am liked by and approved of by everyone.
A fear of making mistakes	– for me to feel good about myself I must never make a mistake, I must be perfect.
Taking the label as all-embracing	– good, bad, stupid, etc.
Believing that being criticised means that I am being rejected	– disapproval of, unloved; affection is withdrawn.

How can we respond assertively?

Decide whether you think the criticism is justified or not – is it *true*?

If it is *untrue*, then express certainty that it isn't true.

It may be based on *false information* (you could say, 'I disagree – the fact is that . . .).

It may be *too broad* – acknowledge what is true and signal disagreement about the generalities.

It may be *judgemental* – in the way an incident is being interpreted. It might be presumed that because you did 'a', then 'b' follows. You need to correct this interpretation.

It may be *person* rather than *behaviour* oriented.

When you've blocked the 'not OK' message, then be self-affirmative (e.g. 'I don't agree, in fact I am very pleased with how I did that').

Above all try to remain positive and concentrate on your strengths.

Giving negative feedback

The guidelines set out in Table 7.4 may be useful when giving negative feedback. (Steps 6 and 7 of Table 7.4 may not be appropriate in all situations.)

Conclusion

The area of feedback is an important one, especially if as a SENCO we want to extend and develop relationships and ideas. While concentrating on the positive, it must be remembered that there will be times for the sake of helping the children with SEN to make progress that the SENCO has to challenge colleagues' perceptions and practices in order to move forward. It is hoped that some of the ideas put forward in this chapter will help SENCOs to achieve this aim.

Table 7.4 Giving negative feedback

Steps 1/2	Check your inner dialogue is sound, and that your criticism is specific, observable. Avoid personalised statements, about attitudes or traits.
Step 3	Set the scene by stating the topic simply before getting into detail. Say why you want to discuss this issue. (e.g. by indicating how it has arisen, by indicating the effects you've noticed on yourself or on the other person's work). Keep it brief.

Step 4	Make your specific criticism. It is your criticism so use 'I' statements:
	    I've noticed that...
	    I think that...
	    I am not satisfied that...
	(not 'people say', 'it as come to my attention', 'it has been noticed that').
	
	Limit the number of criticisms – you can only work on one or two changes at a time. You can explore the effects mentioned briefly in Step 3.

Step 5	Seek agreement – you cannot go to Step 6 unless this is achieved. You will now be checking whether the other person agrees with you, and why the problem occurred. If the person does not agree, there may be valid reasons for seeing things differently. This is the opportunity to uncover new information. You may not have made your expectations clear and this led to the problem – if so, you need to acknowledge your part. At this stage, if this was the difficulty, you need to make your expectations clear and reach agreement that these are realistic.
Step 6	Invite suggestions to bring about change. You may need to make suggestions. Make sure the other person can bring out any difficulties they may feel about this. You may also have to make changes.
Step 7	Summarise what has been agreed, especially what you are *not* going to do. Indicate how and when you will monitor and review the success of the changes.

Chapter 8

Communication skills – making presentations

Another area of communication skills that is central to the SENCO's role is that of effective presentation. Phillips *et al.* (1999) argue that the role carries some responsibility for the professional development of staff, as this is integral to developing and maintaining special educational provision of high quality. They also argue that direct personal intervention in delivery of in-service training is particularly effective when discussing improving school practices and sharing teaching methodologies. Clearly effective presentation skills are beneficial here, although there are many other situations where we need to draw on these skills.

Presentation skills

Presentations can serve a number of *functions*:

– giving information
– receiving information
– problem solving
– training.

Presentations generally *aim to*:

– persuade or sell
– teach
– stimulate thought
– inform.

 Activity 8.1 (see p. 126)
Identifying situations where you may make presentations

In your role as SENCO you are likely to be involved in a range of different presentations, including:

– staff meetings
– teacher education days
– presentations to governors
– introducing speakers
– parents' evenings
– pyramid meetings
– interviews.

Even experienced teachers who make presentations to children every day can become anxious at the prospect of making a presentation to colleagues.

Making presentations involves a wide range of different skills. These skills can be practised and improved. This chapter examines:

- personal presentation skills
- structuring presentations
- the physical environment
- managing groups
- managing individuals.

Structuring a presentation

When you begin to plan a presentation you can write down everything you think of in mind map form, then start to reorganise it in some sort of priority and logical order. This will give you an idea of what information should go where. It may help to start work on the main, or middle, part of the presentation first. Break down your presentation into three elements – 'introduction', 'middle' and 'end'. Your introduction should be approximately 20 per cent of the total presentation, the middle approximately 60 per cent and the end approximately 20 per cent.

Deciding what goes in the introduction

To give you an idea of timing, if you are doing a one-hour presentation, your introduction should last approximately ten to twelve minutes. This may seem rather a long time; however, what you say in your introduction sets the scene for your audience and makes them totally aware of what to expect.

The following should be included in the introduction:

Welcoming courtesies – thanking people for giving their time to attend your presentation and hoping they will feel it is time well spent.

Self-identification – telling people who you are and giving any background information relevant to your presentation. This is also the time to introduce any co-presenters you may have with you.

The objective – what are you proposing to explain, suggest or demonstrate at this presentation. You should angle your objective towards the benefits your audience can expect from what you are about to present. Make sure that your objectives meet those of your audience (why are they there?).

The agenda – tell your audience how long the presentation will last and how it will be broken down, also whether you will be using visual aids to demonstrate particular aspects (video, film, etc.). (See Appendix 3 for further guidance on visual aids.)

Impact – it is also a good idea to have something at the beginning of your presentation to get your audience's attention; something they will be interested in and which will encourage them to listen carefully to you. Using a visual aid to create impact or making an interesting statement will do this, but obviously it needs to be relevant to your presentation.

Range – so that your audience knows exactly what to expect, it is useful to describe the range of areas you will be covering and in what detail. It is also important to explain what will not be covered. Depending on the level of knowledge of your audience, you may decide to go into a limited amount of detail. By explaining this up-front, you leave your audience in no doubt as to what is coming.

Practical details – now is the time to let your audience know if there will be breaks during the presentation and whether they will be given hand-outs or additional information. You should also tell your audience when you would like questions (e.g. at any time during the presentation, or kept until the end).

What goes in the middle?

This is the main part of your presentation and should be approximately 60 per cent of your overall time allocation. If you imagine a presentation to be a 'sandwich', then your beginning and end are the slices of bread, and the middle is all the interesting content.

You need to arrange your content matter into a logical order and make sure it corresponds to the order in which you have introduced it at the beginning.

- You should begin by indicating to your audience what you are firstly going to cover. Talk about it and then concisely summarise what you really want them to remember about the point, before 'flagging' the next area to be presented, and so on.
- It is useful to think of your content areas as small presentations, making sure you introduce them, talk about them and then summarise. This will also help your audience to remember what was said before and how the areas are linked. Try not to make this part too wordy – people remember information better if it is delivered logically and concisely.
- You may need to expand on particular areas of your presentation. This is the place to used examples and illustrations, and also any relevant facts and figures.
- Beware of using too much information at this point – concentrate on getting the information across to meet both your objectives and those of the audience. Too much information will confuse your audience and may mean that they will not remember or understand what is said.

Closing the presentation

You have probably already calculated that around 20 per cent of time has not yet been covered. That is because, like the introduction, the closure of your presentation is very important. You should be careful not just to drift to a halt, but should plan how you are going to finish.

It is useful when planning the ending to revisit your original intention for making the presentation. The objectives set at the beginning should dictate the ending. You should include:

- A concise summary of the salient facts; maybe reintroduce one or two key visual aids to help emphasise the facts.
- What your audience can expect next (e.g. will there be a follow-up

presentation, demonstration, or something else?) Do you need them to do anything with the information?)

- You should give them details of any supporting literature they will be given and an explanation of what it explains and why.
- If you have asked them to raise questions at the end, now is the time to invite these. Some people may need a few seconds to think about any questions they may have – remember to give them 'thinking-time'.
- You should also thank your audience for their attention.

Structure your presentation so that your audience knows where it is going at all times, remember to summarise one section before moving on to the next. Avoid including too much detail, secondary information can be given in hand-out form afterwards.

Delivering your presentation

Only practice can make you a good speaker. Good delivery, apart from a few small (but important) points of technique, is not a question of acquiring skills but of removing obstacles.

Most people speak well enough round a table with a group of friends or colleagues. Learning to speak in public is little more than learning to retain the ability when standing up in front of 10 or 20 or 500 people whom you do not know. This means learning to remove the inhibitions that stop you being your normal, natural, friendly self once you get on your feet!

Get the audience on your side right from the start by making some remark that makes it clear that you are not setting yourself up above the audience and to enlist their sympathetic indulgence rather than risk stimulating a critical resentment.

It is also important to think about how you *sound* (verbal delivery) and *look* (body language).

Verbal delivery
Your voice contributes to the understanding of the message in a variety of ways.

Expression – the amount of emphasis placed on particular words will focus attention on important points. You can show how enthusiastic you are by injecting expression into what you are saying. If you are not enthusiastic about your subject, you can hardly expect the audience to be.

Pausing – do not be afraid of pausing. You do not have to rush through it all like an express train. Give the audience time to take in and digest what you are saying. Certainly, pause after the main points of your presentation.

Be larger than life – you need to use more expression than usual when talking to a large group. Do not be afraid to do this. You have to go quite a long way before you are in danger of going over the top.

Tone of voice and pitch – there is nothing more tedious than listening to a talk delivered in a monotone. A voice that moves up and down like a piano scale is much more interesting. Try practising and listening to your voice with a tape recorder.

Speak clearly – make sure your words do not run into one another. If there are tongue-twisting words in your talk, practise them so that they come out perfectly. You may find you need to speak slightly more slowly than usual.

Speak up – most people give up on a speaker they have to strain to hear. Make sure that you are loud enough for everyone in the room. Practise breathing deeply. Lungs are rather like an organ. If you do not put enough air into them a squeaky sound comes out.

'Illustrate' your talk – talk in pictures to your audience; give them real-life examples to help them make the linkages.

Watch your language – use simple words and short sentences. Avoid using technical terms unless your audience is familiar with them. Never read your presentation from a script – use your prepared cue cards. Keep your head up, not down in your notes.

(Refer to Chapter 3 'Teaching and learning' for more guidance on talking in pictures (visually) and use of language.)

Body language

A quite outstanding contribution to your message is made by all those things you do not actually say: the way you stand; how you are dressed; the gestures you use; whether you look miserable or happy. Unfortunately, in the unnatural environment of speaking to a group, nervous mannerisms can take over: you cannot bear to look at the audience, so you stare at your notes or some point above their heads; you shuffle around or pace up and down. How can you overcome these problems?

Look at the audience – this is essential. You need to look at them to see how they are reacting. You want to worry when the audience stops looking at you for any length of time. This indicates that they are not listening. In small groups you should look at eye-level. If people are arranged in a horseshoe shape, you must make sure you look at the people on the extreme right and left and not just those towards the back. In a large group, the easiest way to maintain eye contact is to 'draw' a large M or W around the room. This will encompass everyone.

Smile – again hard to do if you are quite nervous. Even if you are not particularly happy, smiling can create the illusion of it. It is also surprising how very often the audience smile back. Smiling also has the added benefit of relaxing your vocal chords – it can help to make your voice sound more interesting.

Avoid creating barriers between speaker and audience – you need to get as near to your audience as possible. Standing behind a desk or lectern immediately sets up a barrier. It is always tempting to hide behind something, but it is undesirable.

Stand square – find a comfortable stance. The best position is standing upright with feet slightly apart. Avoid leaning up against a piece of furniture, and keep hands out of pockets.

Beware of distracting mannerisms – this does not mean standing rigid. Most of us use our hands to some extent to add emphasis to what we are saying and we should not stop doing this. However, waving your arms around all over the place is likely to distract the audience. Jangling keys and coins in pockets or wearing clanking jewellery can also distract. The major problem with distracting mannerisms is that if the audience hook on to them, they will concentrate on them rather than listening to your message.

Be natural – easier said than done, but if you concentrate on getting the message across and stop worrying about yourself, you will have more chance of coming over naturally.

Appearance – you should dress to fit the environment you will be delivering in.

Activity 8.2 (see p. 127)
Delivering a presentation – verbal and non-verbal techniques

The choice of venue is important. It really does matter that there should be enough room for the group size, comfortable chairs, adequate heating and ventilation. A good presenter will ensure that the room is set out long before any participants arrive. This communicates a message of control and care to participants. Presenters should ensure that the physical needs of the audience are well looked after (coffee breaks, access to toilets, etc.) One of the most difficult situations is where the presenter does not have control of the venue (e.g. if the presentation is to be made in the school staffroom which is always set out in a certain way).

The physical environment

Even an experienced presenter can be completely thrown by having to deal with a difficult individual in the audience. The best tactic is to anticipate difficulties and think about strategies for dealing with difficult individuals in advance. This ensures that you are not caught on the hop and gives you a feeling of control and confidence. It is worth considering how you would handle the person who:

Dealing with difficult individuals

- moans and casts doom and gloom;
- puts you on the spot with a difficult question;
- does not contribute at all;
- talks when you are talking;
- asks hostile questions;
- monopolises the discussion;
- argues with someone else in the group.

The following *general advice* might be helpful:

- always tackle the problem right away;
- never embarrass a detractor in front of the group;
- never show your anger during a presentation;
- maintain your perspective;
- concentrate on your audience, not yourself;
- use humour;
- remain calm;
- have a 'Plan B';
- project professionalism;
- stay in control;
- confront assertively.

Activity 8.3 (see p. 127)
Dealing with difficult individuals

Group management

Successful presentation is always a two way process which requires the active involvement of the audience. In a formal presentation the audience may simply be required to listen and ask questions. More often, presentations will involve the audience in more activity than this – workshops, small group discussions, carrying out tasks, giving feedback. A useful aphorism to remember is:

> *Tell me and I forget*
> *Show me and I remember*
> *Involve me and I learn*

Managing the active participation of the audience, whether it be managing questions or managing a workshop, can be quite frightening. There is a fine line between the active participation of 40 people and a chaotic rabble. A number of practical questions need to be considered in advance. You need to think about how will you:

- ensure you have the right group size;
- get the attention of the group/get them quiet so you can start;
- ensure the active involvement of the group;
- organise groupwork;
- get a quiet group to contribute;
- deal with questions;
- deal with a hostile audience;
- ensure the whole group takes responsibility for the success of the session;
- get people to return from working groups;
- deal with a group which never produces anything/reaches any agreement;
- motivate a group who are bored;
- work with staff who are tired.

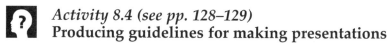 *Activity 8.4 (see pp. 128–129)*
Producing guidelines for making presentations

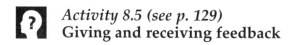 *Activity 8.5 (see p. 129)*
Giving and receiving feedback

Conclusion   Effective presentation skills enable a SENCO to organise and/or deliver in-service training/professional development activities in a confident and competent manner. These skills also help us to be better communicators and to project ourselves in a positive way. These are all skills that facilitate the 'modern SENCO's' role.

Chapter 9

Monitoring and evaluation

In the schools of the twenty-first century the area of review and evaluation is pivotal. The SENCO is charged with monitoring and evaluating the progress that pupils with special educational needs make but this clearly needs to be viewed within a whole-school framework.

A great deal of research has been undertaken into the area of school effectiveness and school improvement with the focus of the school effectiveness work being on the identification and causal measurement of key determinants. Sammons *et al.* (1995) identified 11 factors for effective schools.

Characteristics of effective schools

- Professional leadership.
- Shared vision and goals.
- A learning environment.
- Concentration on teaching and learning.
- Explicit high expectations.
- Positive reinforcement.
- Monitoring progress.
- Pupil rights and responsibilities.
- Purposeful teaching.
- A learning organisation.
- Home–school partnership.

Alongside the area of whole-school development it is clear that the SENCO must work in partnership with subject leaders and heads of department in a consideration of policy and support for children with special needs. In terms of curriculum development and evaluation the following areas have been identified.

Characteristics of effective curriculum areas

- A climate for change.
- A strong vision effectively translated down to the level of the classroom.
- A collegiate management style.
- Good organisation in terms of assessment, record keeping, homework, etc.
- Good resource management.
- An effective system of monitoring and evaluation.

- Structured lessons and regular feedback.
- Clear routines and practices within lessons.
- A syllabus/scheme of work matching the needs and abilities of pupils.
- A strong pupil-centred ethos that systematically rewards pupils.
- Opportunities for autonomous pupil learning.
- A central focus on teaching and learning.

Clearly the needs of all pupils are being considered here but it is helpful to note the emphasis on differentiation that is highlighted. Within the context of their own school the SENCO needs to consider the effectiveness of the provision for special educational needs.

 Activity 9.1 (see p. 129)
Characteristics of effective provision for 'special educational needs'

In determining a school's own success criteria, and while not wanting to undervalue the role of school self review and evaluation, it is important to remember that there is also a role to be undertaken in relation to external accountability. Self evaluation complements inspection with a constant process of identifying priorities for improvement, monitoring provision and evaluating outcomes. *Making Inspection Work for You* (OFSTED 1998) helps schools to see external inspection as one aspect of evaluation, which can actively be used to promote improvement.

The OFSTED context

The OFSTED inspection framework, and the inspectors themselves, recognise the key role played by coordinators in helping to determine and implement the school's objectives.

> Management is to be judged in terms of the extent to which the leadership, as shown by the governing body, headteacher, senior staff and other staff to whom leadership roles have been delegated, promotes quality of learning and standards of achievement.
>
> (OFSTED 1995, p. 100)

The OFSTED framework and schedule (1995) goes on to identify aspects of management:

- Clear objectives and policies focused on pupils' needs.
- Planning and implementation of plans.
- Administration and organisation.
- Effective working relationships.
- Communication within the school.
- Evaluation of performance.
- Clear role definition and appropriate delegation.
- Effective management of finance based on clear priorities.

(We have considered most of these areas in relation to the SENCO in previous chapters.)

The more recent revised Inspection Handbook (OFSTED 1999) builds on these aspects but also includes the area of monitoring, evaluation and the development of teaching. Above all, OFSTED inspectors will want evidence that:

- Teaching is of high quality.
- Learning and progress are taking place.
- Achievement is of high standard.

In particular, the SENCO will clearly be charged with demonstrating the above to OFSTED. In relation to pupils with special needs inspectors will be evaluating how well pupils are doing and the progress they make, particularly towards individual targets which reflect specific needs. They will be concerned with the relationship between practices and SEN policy, with staff awareness of individual need and the need for differentiation, with the purpose and clarity of school procedures, and with liaison with parents and outside agencies. They will clearly also be concerned with the procedures for assessment, recording and reporting and the use made by all staff, including LSAs, of these procedures.

The SENCO will need to have available as much information as possible about the above and while each school will have its own procedures and practices and different inspection teams may emphasise different points, according to school context, it would be beneficial to have the following available:

- the SEN policy;
- the SEN register;
- examples of IEPs , records, samples of pupils work;
- a copy of any school paperwork relevant to SEN (Prospectus, Annual Report to Parents, minutes from governors meetings);
- timetables of support staff or any other relevant timetable information;
- information about links with external agencies;
- any relevant information relating to job descriptions, definitions;
- information about the SEN budget;
- examples of communications with parents;
- details of any relevant parent support meetings;
- details of relevant professional development, both individual and whole staff;
- details of any findings undertaken as a result of self review.

It is important to be as well prepared as possible for the inspection but if the school has been proactive in self review then the outcomes of inspection should not come as too much of a surprise. It is clear however, that the SENCO cannot work in isolation as inspectors will be looking in all classrooms for evidence that the curriculum and teaching strategies meet the needs of all pupils. This is where we stress again the importance of working with all colleagues and with undertaking a professional development role with all staff. As the draft revised Code of Practice (DfEE 2000) reiterates

> The SENCO, with the support of the head teacher and colleagues, seeks to develop effective ways of overcoming barriers to learning and sustaining effective teaching through the analysis and assessment of children's needs, by monitoring the quality of

teaching and standards of pupils' achievement and by setting targets for improvement. (p. 32)

So where might the SENCO begin to undertake monitoring and evaluation? In Chapter 1, the role of the SENCO was examined in some detail, and the descriptions of the role provided by the TTA provide a useful starting point for reviewing and evaluating the *management* of special educational provision within a school. To recap, the TTA (1998) describe the SENCO's *core purpose* as follows:

The SENCO, with the support of the head teacher and governing body, takes responsibility for the day-to-day operation of provision made by the school for pupils with SEN and provides professional guidance in the area of SEN in order to secure high quality teaching and the effective use of resources to bring about improved standards of achievement for all pupils.

The SENCO's fundamental task is to support the head teacher in ensuring that all staff recognise the importance of planning their lessons in ways that will encourage the participation and learning of all pupils. The SENCO should seek to ensure, through active collaboration with subject leaders, that the learning of all pupils is given equal priority, and that available resources are used efficiently in support of this purpose. The SENCO plays a key role in supporting, guiding and motivating colleagues, particularly in disseminating examples of effective practice in relation to pupils with SEN.

Working with the head teacher, staff, parents, the governing body and other agencies, the SENCO co-ordinates the day-to-day operation of the SEN policy, ensuring that the name of any pupil identified as a cause for concern, including those with behavioural problems, is entered on the SEN register and then is appropriately followed through in terms of the Code of Practice suggested procedures. The SENCO keeps the head teacher informed of the operation of the policy and develops effective working relationships with parents.

Additionally, the 'four areas of SEN coordination', which were first introduced in Chapter 1, can help SENCOs to focus on particular aspects of provision which should be monitored and evaluated. These can be found as photocopiable pages at the back of the book and as downloadable electronic files from www.fultonpublishers.co.uk

Definition of terms

It is helpful at this point to consider exactly what we mean by some of the terms commonly used in this area.

Monitoring – is checking what is happening and the extent to which things have gone according to plan. This could be administrative (budgets, attendance on courses) or professional (strengths and weaknesses, activities provided and received as planned).

Evaluation – is the collection, analysis, discussion and reporting of evidence which allows judgements to be made about whether we are being successful or not.

These two activities are closely linked and provide evidence to serve two purposes:

Accountability – demonstrating that resources are being properly deployed to maintain and improve standards.

Development – assisting in the formative process of improving teaching and learning through curriculum development.

In many cases schools are becoming more effective at monitoring, where they may for example examine pupils' work to see if the curriculum is being covered. It can be more difficult to evaluate, as here we require a judgement to be made about the success or otherwise of a process or action and this might clearly involve having to feedback an element of unsatisfactory performance to a colleague.

 Activity 9.2 (see p. 130)
Identifying monitoring and evaluating provision

As mentioned previously it is also important to monitor and evaluate the *quality of teaching and learning* which pupils receive, as well as the management of time. The following extracts from Landy and Gains (1996) provide one example of how this might be undertaken.

Pupil responses: Key questions on the quality of learning

- What is the quality of learning taking place in this school?
- Is the learning at an appropriate pace?
- Are pupils gaining in knowledge, understanding and skills?
- What is their ability in reading, writing, numeracy and oracy?
- Does the pupils' attainment meet or exceed that expected for their ages?
- Are opportunities provided for observation and information seeking?
- Are pupils given the chance to look for patterns and deeper understanding?
- Are they encouraged to pose questions and solve problems?
- Can they apply their knowledge in unfamiliar situations?
- Are they involved in evaluating their own work and do they reflect on it and link it with past experience?
- Do they demonstrate the ability to concentrate and partake in sustained activities?
- Do they cooperate with each other?
- Are they sufficiently motivated?
- Do they respond to the challenges set by teachers with confidence, appropriate attitudes and adaptability?
- Are the pupils making progress and how can this be demonstrated? For example:

Records of achievement
Past records and reports to parents
Named, dated examples of work over time
Video evidence of progress
Schools' self analysis and review procedures
Targets achieved in IEPs

Annual review reports
Parents' and pupils' comments and perceptions.

Key questions on the quality of teaching
In a similar way to assessing the quality of learning, inspectors will comment on the quality of teaching. Key questions here will include:

- Were appropriate goals set for whole classes, groups and individuals?
- Were the activities planned and well presented?
- Is the content appropriate and motivating?
- Was the organisation and management effective?
- Was a range of teaching skills in evidence?
- Was the pace appropriate?
- Could progression and rigour be demonstrated?
- Was there feedback to the students?
- How was the work monitored or evaluated?
- What was the quality of any support assistants or teachers?
- Were the pupil groupings suitable?
- Was the subject well covered with a clear command and secure knowledge base?
- Was there evidence of differentiation and planning to meet individual needs?
- Were resources well planned, organised and used?
- Were the expectations and standards achieved appropriate?

The OFSTED Handbook (OFSTED 1999, p. 150) suggests that there are four questions at the heart of evaluation:

- Are all the pupils in my school learning as much as they are capable of learning?
- What can I do to find out?
- When I answer the question how do I know I am right?
- What do I do about it when I have the answer?

If a system for monitoring and evaluation is in place already in the school it is perhaps easier to undertake a review of teaching and learning within classrooms. If not, it is essential to negotiate carefully the intended focus, and begin in a small way. It is important to choose the most appropriate focus and think carefully about the process. The following may act as a starting point.

Face to face contact

- Showing sensitive awareness of, for example, informal comments made in the staffroom which point to a need for discussions with individual teachers on particular issues.
- Group/departmental discussions.
- Interviews – appraisal/professional development.

Active participation

- Joining colleagues for a degree of collaborative teaching.
- Joining colleagues in the classroom in order to consider a particular aspect of curricular provision, teaching strategies, resource allocation and usage.
- Involvement in meetings, discussions, workshops.

Correspondence

- Tick in box questionnaire.
- Structured free response questionnaire.
- Open-ended questionnaire.

Objective measures

- Teacher performance indicators.
- Pupil performance indicators.
- Records.
- Observation schedules.
- OFSTED criteria.

Scrutiny of documentation

- Records.
- Pupils' work – folios/portfolios.
- Policies and guidelines.

What kind of evidence do I need in order to monitor?

Monitoring is only as good as the quality of the information on which it is based.

> **Documentary evidence** – schemes of work, timetables, information, DfEE/LEA guidelines, texts, exercise books, etc.
> **Observational evidence** – what is seen by the observer in the classroom, in groupwork, etc.
> **Evidence from people** – what they have observed, their opinions, judgements, experiences.

We need to remember that what we are gaining here involves two very different types of evidence, often referred to as 'soft' and 'hard' data. Hard data would be usually taken from documentary evidence and soft data would concern evidence from people. Soft data is sometimes judged to be less valid because it is concerned with interpretation of others' actions or opinions but it can provide alternative perspectives. It is probably useful to include a combination of both types.

 Activity 9.3 (see p. 130)
Monitoring aspects of teaching and learning

An approach to monitoring.

It is worth considering four steps to effective monitoring (Figure 9.1).

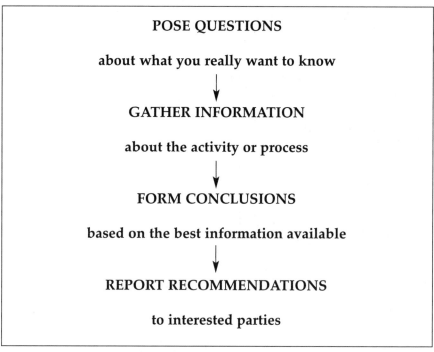

POSE QUESTIONS

about what you really want to know

GATHER INFORMATION

about the activity or process

FORM CONCLUSIONS

based on the best information available

REPORT RECOMMENDATIONS

to interested parties

Figure 9.1 Four steps to effective monitoring

Each SENCO will need to decide:

- The key things to monitor and evaluate (and how much to do).
- The monitoring structure and who will be involved (head teacher, other staff, pupils, governors, LEA, etc.).
- The success criteria.
- Who will provide the information.
- Who will be responsible.
- The time-scale.
- The means for obtaining a balance of external/internal views.
- What will be done with the information.

Figure 9.2 shows the key questions in monitoring.

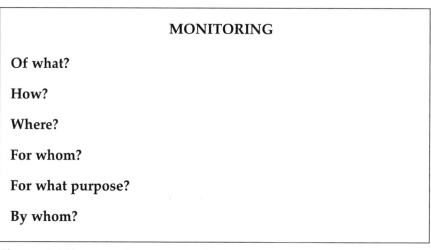

MONITORING

Of what?

How?

Where?

For whom?

For what purpose?

By whom?

Figure 9.2 Key questions in monitoring

It is essential that the SENCO works with others responsible for the SEN policy in deciding on a focus, especially if classroom observation is to be a vehicle that is drawn upon. Staff need to know exactly what the observer is trying to establish when they are observing classroom practice. Below are some possible focus areas.

Classroom observation

Possible focus areas:

1. **Resources**
   - availability
   - selection
   - suitability
   - accessibility to pupils/location/rules of use
   - match to task

2. **Questioning**
   - to motivate and stimulate
   - to test recollection
   - to widen reference
   - to direct

3. **Differentiation**
   - by means of questioning
   - by means of vocabulary
   - be means of content
   - by means of expectation
   - by means of talk
   - by means of apparatus
   - by means of goal setting

4. **Time management**
   - are pupils having a fair share of teacher time?

5. **Grouping of pupils**
   - composition of group
   - size of groups
   - number of groups
   - access to resources
   - movement around the room
   - accepted procedures
   - number of activities

6. **Class control**
   - rewards
   - sanctions

7. **Relationships**
   - pupil/pupil
   - teacher/pupil
   - adult/pupil

8. **Assessment**
   - strategies
   - feedback
   - records

9. **Integration of IT**

Governing bodies and head teachers will need to give careful thought to a SENCO's timetable in the light of these responsibilities. Clearly evaluation should not be undertaken without considerable thought to the areas of focus and the dissemination of the findings. There may well be a major staff development role to be undertaken as a result.

Class-level evaluation alone will not improve schools. There needs to be a commitment to study the evidence gained, to scrutinise the data, to 'make sense' of it and to plan and act differently as a result. The new OFSTED (1999) inspection framework focuses much more on schools' analysis of data on how well different groups of children are performing.

In the current climate there is still a culture of 'initiative overload' and it is hoped that firm and purposeful leaders will be able to adopt a participative approach to school improvement. Nowhere is this more crucial than in the leadership role of the SENCO who is constantly being asked to lead change and initiate improvement.

Summary

The SENCO clearly holds a central role in school improvement and this has not always been recognised by schools in the past. It is helpful therefore to note that the revised draft Code of Practice (DfEE 2000) addresses this issue in part by recommending that the SENCO should form part of the senior management team of a school.

In the twenty-first century schools are undoubtedly facing the challenge posed by the worldwide philosophy of inclusive schooling and the rights of all children to receive education in a mainstream environment. It is the SENCO who finds himself or herself the key player in making inclusion work and in forging meaningful links with SEN specialists in order to provide the highest quality education for all pupils.

It has been our intention throughout this book to highlight the important role of the SENCO as manager as well as teacher and we hope that we have stimulated thinking in that area. Improving the quality of teaching and learning for all pupils is a central aim and one which undoubtedly takes considerable time and patience. The process of change in meeting individual needs will continue and the SENCO will remain at the heart of it. We hope that we have provided some insights into strategies that can enable SENCOs and their pupils to achieve success.

Appendix 1

Sample IEP for Child in Year 2

Stage 2 Action (No. 1)

Priority areas	Targets			
1. Reading Skills – letter sounds – sight words	Know the sounds l, h, n, y Read: look, here, no yes (360 scheme) accurately and consistently			
2. Visual Skills – can repeat sequences of 2 at present	Sequence patterns of 3 items			
3. Language Skills – can only securely follow 2 instructions	Follow 3 instructions first thing in the morning and 3 instructions in classwork.			
Action to be taken	**Resources/Methods/ Frequency/Duration/ Group size**	**Person/s responsible**	**Signed**	**Date**
1. Take letter sound and word home to learn during the week.	360 Reading Scheme Level 1	Mrs Brown Mrs Platt		July
2. Sequence beads, pictures, counters, cubes, etc.	SEN Time Easy Learn, 'Order order' etc.	Mrs Platt		
3. Before register 2 → 3 set things to do. Work with Mrs Platt – 2 → 3 instructions in work	Teacher's own as appropriate	Mrs Platt		Review December

Appendix 2

Individual Education Plan

Curriculum Support

Name _____

Form/Group _____

Targets	English	Maths	Science	Science	PSE	Technology	MFL	History	Geography	RE	IT	Music	Art	PE	

Appendix 3

Planning and using visual aids

There are two basic rules:

- A visual aid must be necessary
- It must be visual.

Remember the following

1. Plan when/how to use your visuals – but never rely on them totally. If the worst happened and your projector didn't work, you should still be able to make your presentation.
2. Keep your visuals simple – simplify the information to be presented. Never use columns of facts and figures – put this information into a pie-chart or bar-graph. This will help your audience to understand the data.
3. Allow time for your audience to look at the visuals – do not talk and show visuals at the same time. Never leave a visual on show – don't leave you audience looking at something which doesn't relate to what you are now saying.
4. Do not use visuals just for the sake of it – limit the number you use, and don't use too may different types of visuals. For example, stick to a flip chart and overhead projector only. Don't use every method in one presentation as it will become too busy and confusing for both you and your audience.
5. Never turn your back on your audience; talk to them not to the screen, point to the actual projector and not the screen.
6. Make sure everyone can see your visual aids – if using flip charts or overhead slides use colour and large bold letters and pictures.
7. Visual aids are mainly to help the audience and not the presenter.
8. Before making your presentation, check any equipment to be used. Make sure you have extension leads, spare pens, etc.
9. All visuals should be professionally prepared – they must look good, but this doesn't always mean they have to be expensive.
10. Always have a practice run through your presentation using the visual aids. They can add time to your overall presentation.

Appendix 4

Giving and receiving feedback – checklist

It is important that you give constructive feedback on each presentation. (See Chapter 7 to help you cover the main points, using the headings below.)

Name of presenter

Topic

Structure

Was there evidence of planning?

Was the purpose/objective clear?

Did it seem well structured?

Visual aids

Were visual aids helpful and clear?

Delivery

Comment on tone of voice and articulation

Were mannerisms and gestures helpful or obstructive?

Was good eye contact maintained?

Did the speaker maintain an interesting pace?

Bibliography

Ainscow, M. (1993) 'Teacher development and special educational needs', in Mitler, P. *et al.* (eds) *Special Needs Education (World Yearbook of Education)*. London: Kogan Page.

Back, K. and Back, K. (1982) *Assertiveness at Work*. London: Mcgraw Hill.

Bar-Tal, D. *et al.* (1980) 'The relationship between locus of control and academic achievement, anxiety and level of aspiration', *British Journal of Educational Psychology* **31**, 482–90.

Bender, W. N. (1995) *Learning Disabilities: Characteristics, identification and teaching strategies*, 2nd edn. Boston: Allyn and Bacon.

Bennett, N. (1991) 'The quality of classroom learning experiences for children with special educational needs', in Ainscow, M. (ed.) *Effective Schools for All*. London: David Fulton Publishers.

Berger, A. and Gross, J. (1999) *Teaching the Literacy Hour in an Inclusive Classroom*. London : David Fulton Publishers.

Booth, T. *et al.* (2000) *Index for Inclusion*. Bristol: Centre for Studies in Inclusive Education (CSIE).

Burns, R. B. (1982) *The Self Concept: Theory, measurement, development and behaviour*. London: Longman.

Byers, R. and Rose, R. (1996) *Planning the Curriculum for Pupils with Special Educational Needs*. London: David Fulton Publishers.

Carpenter, B. *et al.* (1996) *Enabling Access*. London: David Fulton Publishers.

Charlton, T. (1986) 'A special need in the curriculum: education for life', in Charlton, T. *et al.* (eds) *Educating Children with Learning and Behaviour Problems some considerations*. Faculty of Education Monograph No. 1. Cheltenham: College of St Paul and St Mary.

Charlton, T. (1992) 'Giving access to the National Curriculum by working on the "self"', in Jones, K. and Charlton, T. (eds) *Learning Difficulties in Primary Classrooms: Delivering the whole curriculum*. London: Routledge.

Charlton, T. and David, K. (1996) *Pastoral Care Matters in Primary and Middle Schools*. London, Routledge.

Charlton, T. and George, J. (1993) 'The development of problem behaviours', in *Managing Misbehaviour in Schools*, 2nd edn. London: Routledge.

Charlton, T. *et al.* (1996) 'The effects of teacher behaviour upon pupil behaviour', in Charlton, T. *et al.* (eds) *Pupil Needs and Classroom Practices*. Cheltenham: Park Published Papers.

Cooper, P. (1996) 'Pupils as partners: pupils contributions to the government of schools', in Jones, K. and Charlton, T. (eds) *Overcoming Learning and Behaviour Difficulties: Partnership with pupils*. London: Routledge.

Cooper, P. and Ideus, K. (1996) *Attention Deficit/Hyperactivity Disorder: A practical guide for teachers*. London: David Fulton Publishers.

Crew, J. and Woodcock, E. (1996) 'ADHD – don't just cope, learn to manage', – in Jones, K. *et al.* (eds) *Pupils Needs and Classroom Practices*. Cheltenham: Park Published Papers.

Croll, P. and Moses, D. (1985) *One in Five*. London: Routledge.

DES (Department of Education and Science) (1978) *Special Educational Needs: Report of the Committee of Inquiry into the education of handicapped children and young people* (The Warnock Report). London: HMSO.

DFE (Department for Education) (1993) *The Education Act*. London: HMSO.

DFE (1994) *Code of Practice for the Identification and Assessment of Special Educational Needs*. London: HMSO.

DfEE (Department for Education and Employment) (1997a) *The SENCO Guide – Good practice for SENCOs*. London: HMSO.

DfEE (1997b) *Excellence for All Children – Meeting special educational needs*. London: HMSO.

DfEE (1998) *Meeting Special Educational Needs. A programme of action*. London: HMSO.

DfEE (1999) *Additional Literacy Strategy*. London: HMSO.

DfEE (2000) *SEN Code of Practice on the Identification and Assessment of Special Educational Needs. Consultation*. London: DfEE.

Dyson, A. and Gains, G. (1995) 'The role of the special educational needs coordinator. Poisoned chalice or crock of gold?' *Support for Learning* **10**(2), 50–6.

Epstein, M. H. *et al.* (1977) 'Impulsive cognitive tempo in severe and mild learning disabled children', *Psychology in the Schools* **14**, 290–4.

Galloway, D. (1985) *Schools, Pupils and Special Educational Needs*. Beckenham: Croom Helm.

Gardner, H. (1993) *Multiple Intelligences. The Theory in Practice*. New York: Basic Books.

Gross, J. (1993) *Special Educational Needs in the Primary School – A practical guide*. Buckingham: Open University Press.

Gross, J. (2000) 'Paper promises? Making the Code work for you', *Support for Learning* **15**(3), 126–33.

Haylock, D. W. (1991) *Teaching Mathematics to Low Attainers, 8–12*. London: Paul Chapman Publishers.

Hereford and Worcester Council (1994) *Guidelines for Schools – The Code of Practice for children with special educational needs*. Hereford and Worcester Council.

Hughes, M. (1999) *Closing the Learning Gap*. Stafford: Network Educational Press.

Ideus, K. (1991) 'Cultural foundations of ADHD: a sociological analysis.' *Therapeutic Care and Education* **3**(2), 111–29.

Jones, K. (1992) 'Recognising successes and difficulties in learning', in Jones, K. and Charlton, T. (eds) *Learning Difficulties in Primary Classrooms: Delivering the Whole Curriculum*. London: Routledge.

Jones, K. and Charlton, T. (1996) 'Sources of learning and behaviour difficulties', in Jones, K. and Charlton, T. (eds) *Overcoming Learning and Behaviour Difficulties: Partnership with pupils.* London: Routledge.

Jones, K. and Lock, M. (1993) 'Working with parents', in Charlton, T. and David, K. (eds) *Managing Misbehaviour in Schools*, 2nd edn. London: Routledge.

Jones, K. and Quah, M. (1996) ' The professional development needs of learning support coordinators in Singapore', *European Journal of Special Needs Education* 5.

Jones, K. *et al.* (1996) 'Supporting learning within the classroom', in Jones, K. and Charlton, T. (eds) *Overcoming Learning and Behaviour Difficulties: Partnership with pupils.* London: Routledge.

Lambley, H. (1993) 'Learning and behaviour problems', in Charlton, T. and David, K. (eds) *Managing Misbehaviour in Schools*, 2nd edn. London: Routledge.

Landy, M. and Gains, C. (1996) *Inspecting Special Needs Provision in Schools.* London: David Fulton Publishers.

Lewis, J. (1996) 'Helping children to find a voice', in Jones, K. and Charlton, T. (eds) *Overcoming Learning and Behaviour Difficulties: Partnership with pupils.* London: Routledge.

Maistervitale, B. (1987) *Unicorns are Real. A right brained approach to learning.* California: Jalmar Press.

Mortimore, P. *et al.* (1998) *School Matters in Primary and Middle Schools.* London: Routledge.

Oaklander, V. (1997) 'Windows to our children – a gestalt therapy approach to children and adolescents', *Gestalt Journal.* New York: (Highland).

OFSTED (1995) *Handbook for Inspecting Schools.* London: HMSO.

OFSTED (1998) *Making Inspection Work for You.* London: HMSO.

OFSTED (1999) *Handbook for Inspecting Primary and Nursery Schools.* London: HMSO.

Phillips, S. *et al.* (1999) *Management Skills for SEN Coordinators in the Primary School.* London: Falmer Press.

QCA (1998) 'Factors relating to curriculum provision which are common amongst excluded pupils'. An unpublished report of research undertaken by the Centre for Special Education, University College Worcester in association with the Centre of Behaviour Studies, Cheltenham and Gloucester College of Education, on behalf of the Qualifications and Curriculum Authority.

QCA (Qualifications and Curriculum Authority) (2000) *The National Curriculum Handbook. Handbook for primary teachers in England.* London: DfEE.

Reynolds, D. (1984) 'Creative conflict: the implications of recent educational research for those concerned with children', *Maladjustment and Therapeutic Education* **2**(1), 14–18.

Rose, C. (1985) *Accelerated Learning.* New York: Bantan Doubleday Dell Publishing Group.

Sammons, P. *et al.* (1995) *Key Characteristics of Effective Schools.* London: OFSTED.

Scott-Bauman, A. (1996) 'Listen to the child', in Jones, K. and Charlton, T. (eds) *Overcoming Learning and Behaviour Difficulties: Partnership with pupils*. London: Routledge.

Smith, A. (1998) *Accelerated Learning in Practice*. Stafford: Network Educational Press.

Smith, A. (1996) *Accelerated Learning in the Classroom*. Stafford: Network Educational Press.

Smith, C. R. (1994) *Learning Disabilities: The interaction of the learner, task and setting*, 3rd edn. Boston: Allyn and Bacon.

Smith, D. (1993) *Powerful Presentation Skills*. Boulder: Career Track Publications.

Szwed, C. (1997) 'The role of the special educational needs coordinator' (unpublished dissertation), University of Coventry.

TTA (Teacher Training Agency) (1998) *National Standards for Special Educational Needs Coordinators*. London: TTA.

TTA (1999) *National Special Educational Needs Specialist Standards*. London: TTA.

Temple, S. (1996) 'Non-directive counselling in schools', in Jones, K. and Charlton, T. (eds) *Overcoming Learning and Behaviour Difficulties: Partnership with pupils*. London: Routledge.

Thomas, A., and Chess, S. (1997) *Temperament and Development*. New York: Bruner/Mazel.

Tisdall, G. and Dawson, R. (1994) 'Listening to children: interviews with children attending a mainstream supporting faculty'. *Support for Learning* 9(4), 179–82.

Topping, K. (1991) 'Achieving more with less: raising reading standards with parental involvement and peer tutoring', *Support for Learning* 6(3), 112–15.

Tyler, S. (1990) 'Subtypes of specific learning difficulties: a review', in Pumfrey, P. D. and Elliott, C. D. (eds) *Children's Difficulties in Reading, Writing, and Spelling*. London: Falmer Press.

UNESCO (1993) *Special Needs in the Classroom*. Paris: UNESCO.

Wade, B. and Moore, M. (1993) *Experiencing Special Education*. Buckingham: Open University Press.

Walden, T. A. and Ramey, C. T. (1983) 'Locus of control and academic achievement: results from a pre-school programme', *Journal of Educational Psychology* 75(3), 347–58.

Walker, N. W. (1985) 'Impulsivity in learning disabled children: past research findings and methodological inconsistencies', *Learning Disability Quarterly* 8, 85–94.

Webb, G. M. (1983) 'Left/right brains, team-mates in learning', *Exceptional Children* 49, 508–15.

Westwood, P. (1993) *Commonsense Methods for Children with Special Educational Needs*. London: Routledge.

Wolfendale, S. (1986) 'Involving pupils in behavioural management: a whole-school approach', *Support for Learning* 1(4), 32–8.

Activities*

Objectives

Part One of this book has been designed to enable you to:

- place policy and practice in the context of current perspectives on special educational needs (SEN);
- assess the needs of pupils identified as having SEN;
- formulate and effectively manage Individual Education Plans (IEPs);
- put into practice effective teaching for pupils with SEN.

Part One: Managing learning – Activities

Objectives

Chapter 1 has been designed to enable you to:

(a) examine the concept of 'special educational needs';
(b) describe the range of factors which cause successes and difficulties in learning;
(c) analyse the complementary roles of class/subject teachers and the SENCO in relation to (b) above;
(d) examine the relationship between (a), (b) and (c) above and recent legislation/guidance concerning the implementation of the *Code of Practice for the Identification and Assessment of Special Educational Needs*, the SENCO standards and the revised National Curriculum.

Chapter 1: The role of the SENCO – Activities

Activity 1.1
Perceptions of special educational needs

Write down a definition of 'special educational needs' which you could present to a child's parent(s)/carers at your first meeting with them. Record that definition in the space below so that you can reflect upon it later.

Ask two colleagues how they might define the term 'special educational needs' to parents/carers. Record their responses and compare them with your own definition.

First colleague's definition of *special educational needs*

Second colleague's definition of *special educational needs*

www.fultonpublishers.co.uk

Activity 1.2
Identifying the 'special' in special educational needs

Ask a colleague to describe the 'special educational needs' of a pupil who is known to them. Record a summary of their description below.

To what extent does that account of a pupil's 'special educational needs' emphasise the need for some kind of 'different' or 'additional' provision?

A colleague's description of a particular child's special educational needs

Notes on the provision which is actually made for that child. Consider whether the provision equates to the perception above of the child's 'special need'.

www.fultonpublishers.co.uk

103

Activity 1.3
Assessing a pupil's special educational needs – who can contribute?

Using the following table, consider the contributions which class/subject teachers, learning support assistants, SENCOs, pupils and parents could make to the assessment of a particular learner's special educational needs.

	The **class/subject teacher** could contribute information about:	A **learning support assistant** could contribute information about:	The **SENCO** could contribute information about:	The **pupil** could contribute information about:	The **parents** could contribute information about:
Factors within **the learner**					
Factors within **the curriculum**					
Factors within **the learning environment**					

www.fultonpublishers.co.uk

Activity 1.4
Identifying the professional development needs of the teaching staff in your school in relation to special educational needs

The immediate professional development needs of teaching staff

1.

2.

The long term needs of the teaching staff

1.

2.

www.fultonpublishers.co.uk

Activity 1.5
What is the role of the SENCO?

On the basis of what you have read so far, consider and provide brief responses to the following questions.

What is a coordinator?

What is a special educational needs coordinator?

What skills does a SENCO need?

How does he/she acquire and develop those skills?

Who/what can help?

How can the SENCO effect change to improve the school's provision for SEN?

Who else should be involved in effecting and sustaining improvement?

www.fultonpublishers.co.uk

Activity 1.6
Auditing provision, setting priorities and formulating your school's action plan

1. The four key areas of SEN coordination are detailed here.
2. In the boxes alongside each item (below) indicate those aspects which you need to work upon and the date by which you hope to implement developments within each area.

Four key areas of SEN coordination

A. *Strategic direction and development of SEN provision in the school*

SENCOs coordinate, with the support of the head teacher and within the context of the school's aims and policies, the development and implementation of the SEN policy in order to raise achievement and improve the quality of education provided. They:

		Tick areas to be worked on	Date for implement-ation
i	contribute effectively to the development of a positive ethos in which all pupils have access to a broad, balanced and relevant curriculum and which contributes to pupils' spiritual, moral, cultural, mental and physical development and in preparing pupils for the opportunities, responsibilities and experiences of adult life;		
ii	support staff in understanding the learning needs of pupils with SEN and the importance of raising their achievement;		
iii	ensure that the objectives of the SEN policy are reflected in the school development plan, that effective systems are in place to identify and meet needs and that they are coordinated, monitored, evaluated and reviewed;		
iv	monitor the progress made in setting objectives and targets for pupils with SEN, assist in the evaluation of the effectiveness of teaching and learning, and use the analysis to guide further improvement;		
v	advise the head teacher and governing body on the level of resources required to maximise the achievements of pupils with SEN;		
vi	liaise with and coordinate the contribution of external agencies;		
vii	analyse and interpret relevant national, local and school data plus research and inspection evidence to inform the SEN policy, practices and expectations, targets and teaching methods.		

www.fultonpublishers.co.uk

B. *Teaching and learning*

SENCOs seek to develop, with the support of the head teacher and colleagues, effective ways of overcoming barriers to learning and sustaining effective teaching through the analysis and assessment of pupils' needs, by monitoring the quality of teaching and standards of pupils' achievements, and by setting targets for improvement. They:

		Tick areas to be worked on	Date for implement-ation
i	support the identification of, and disseminate, the most effective teaching approaches for pupils with SEN;		
ii	collect and interpret specialist assessment data gathered on pupils and use it to inform practice;		
iii	work with pupils, subject leaders and class teachers with tutorial/pastoral responsibilities to ensure that realistic expectations of behaviour and achievements are set for pupils with SEN;		
iv	monitor the effective use of resources, appropriate teaching and learning activities and target-setting to meet the needs of pupils with SEN;		
v	develop systems for monitoring and recording progress made by pupils with SEN towards the achievement of targets set;		
vi	support the development of improvements in literacy, numeracy and information technology skills, as well as access to the wider curriculum;		
vii	identify and develop study skills to support pupils in their ability to work independently and learn more effectively;		
viii	support other staff in developing pupils' understanding of the duties, opportunities, responsibilities and rights of citizens;		
ix	know how to recognise and deal with stereotyping in relation to disability or race;		
x	maintain effective partnerships between parents and school's staff so as to promote pupils' learning; provide information to parents about targets, achievements and progress;		
xi	develop effective liaison between schools to ensure that there is good continuity in terms of support and progression in learning when pupils with SEN transfer;		
xii	develop effective liaison with external agencies in order to provide maximum support for pupils with SEN.		

www.fultonpublishers.co.uk

C. *Leading and managing staff*

SENCOs support staff involved in working with pupils with SEN by ensuring all those involved have the information necessary to secure improvements in teaching and learning and sustain staff motivation. They:

		Tick areas to be worked on on	Date for implement-ation
i	help staff to achieve constructive working relationships with pupils with SEN;		
ii	encourage all members of staff to recognise and fulfil their statutory responsibilities to pupils with SEN;		
iii	ensure the establishment of opportunities for the SENCO, learning support assistants and other teachers to review the needs, progress and targets of pupils with SEN;		
iv	provide regular information to the head teacher and governing body on the evaluation of the effectiveness of provision for pupils with SEN, to inform decision making and policy review;		
v	advise, contribute to and, where appropriate, coordinate the professional development of staff to increase their effectiveness in responding to pupils with SEN, and provide support and training to trainee and newly qualified teachers in relation to the standards of Qualified Teacher Status, Career Entry Profiles and standards for induction.		

D. *Efficient and effective deployment of staff and resources*

SENCOs identify, with the support of the head teacher and governing body, appropriate resources to support the teaching of pupils with SEN and monitor their use in terms of efficiency, effectiveness and safety. They:

		Tick areas to be worked on on	Date for implement-ation
i	establish staff and resource requirements to meet the needs of pupils with SEN, advise the head teacher, senior management team and governing body of likely priorities for expenditure, and allocate resources made available with maximum efficiency to meet the objectives of the school and SEN policies, and to achieve value for money;		
ii	deploy, or advise the head teacher on the deployment of staff involved in working with pupils with SEN to ensure the most efficient use of teaching and other expertise;		
iii	organise and coordinate the deployment of learning resources, including information and communications technology, and monitor their effectiveness;		
iv	maintain existing resources and explore opportunities to develop or incorporate new resources from the wide range of sources inside and outside the school.		

www.fultonpublishers.co.uk

Activity 1.7
Identifying the SENCO's professional development needs

1. In the light of your responses to Activities 1.5 and 1.6 and the TTA's 1998 Key Outcomes (*National Standards for Special Educational Needs Coordinators*) list, in order of priority, your immediate professional development needs regarding your role as a SENCO.
2. Amend your responses to Activity 1.4 in the light of the four key areas and the Key Outcomes identified by the TTA (1998).

My professional development needs (as a SENCO) in order of priority:

1.

2.

3.

4.

www.fultonpublishers.co.uk

Objectives

This chapter has been designed to enable you to:

(a) examine the concept and context of an Individual Education Plan (IEP);
(b) formulate an effective IEP;
(c) consider the role of support staff;
(d) evaluate the success of the IEP.

Chapter 2:
Planning for
special needs –
Activities

Activity 2.1
What is the purpose of an IEP?

In the space provided write down what you perceive as the purpose of an IEP.

The purpose of an IEP

Activity 2.2
Who may contribute to the IEP?

- Identify a child for whom you will be drawing up an IEP. Focus on one priority concern.
- Identify who, in addition to the SENCO, should be involved in planning the IEP. Note any obstacles to including them and any solutions or factors which you may need to pursue such as the need for time to work with other adults, accommodation for consultation, liaison with key individuals such as the child himself, parents, SEN governor, support teacher, etc.

www.fultonpublishers.co.uk

Contributors	Knowledge and skills	Obstacles?	Solutions/actions
1.			
2.			
3.			

Activity 2.3
Making effective use of support staff

Consider how your learning support assistant/support assistant team can contribute in implementing the IEP for the child identified in Activity 2.2.

Support assistant's contribution

www.fultonpublishers.co.uk

Objectives

Chapter 3 has been designed to enable you to:

(a) analyse the range of learning styles, intelligences and affective factors (e.g. self-concept and locus of control) which must be taken into account when planning special educational provision;

(b) plan educational experiences which best meet the individual learning requirements of all pupils.

Chapter 3:
Teaching and
learning –
Activities

Activity 3.1
Identifying your preferred learning style

Identify your preferred style of learning by carrying out the following activity devised by Colin Rose (1985). Circle or highlight the boxes which apply to you.

When you		Visual	Auditory	Kinaesthetic
Spell	*do you*	try to see the word	use the phonetic approach	write the word down to find if it 'feels' right
Visualise	*do you*	see vivid detailed pictures	think in sounds	have few images, those that you do have involve movement
Concentrate	*do you*	get distracted by untidiness or movement	get distracted by sounds/noises	get distracted by movement
Are angry	*do you*	become silent and seethe	express it in an outburst	storm off, grit your teeth, clench your fists
Forget something	*do you*	forget names but remember faces	forget faces but remember names	remember best what you did
Contact people on business	*do you*	prefer a direct, personal meeting face to face	prefer the telephone	talk it out while walking or during another activity
Are relaxing	*do you*	prefer to watch TV, read, see a play	prefer to listen to the radio/play music tapes, CDs	prefer to play sport/games
Enjoy the arts	*do you*	like paintings	like music	like dancing
Reward someone	*do you*	write remarks of praise on their work in a note	give them oral praise	give them a pat on the back
Try to interpret someone's mood	*do you*	primarily look at their facial expression	listen to their tone of voice	watch their body movements
Are reading	*do you*	like descriptive scenes/stop to imagine the scene/take little notice of pictures	enjoy dialogue and conversation and 'hear' the characters talk	prefer action stories or are not a keen reader
Learn	*do you*	like to see demonstrations, diagrams, slides, posters	like verbal instructions, talks and lectures	prefer direct involvement – learning through activities/role playing etc.
Are inactive	*do you*	look around, doodle, watch something	talk to yourself or other people	fidget
Are talking	*do you*	talk sparingly, but dislike listening for too long	enjoy listening but are impatient to talk	gesture a lot and use expressive movements

www.fultonpublishers.co.uk

Activity 3.2
Modality preferences and planning provision

Imagine a child with a similar pattern of modality preferences to you. If you had to advise a colleague on how best to teach that child to spell, what strategies would you recommend. Record your answer in the space below.

Recommended spelling strategy

Activity 3.3
Preferred intelligences

Complete the following chart as it relates to yourself. Grade each item on a 0 – 5 scale (where 5 refers to a high degree of competency and 0 refers to no competency). On the following page transfer the outcomes to the list of seven intelligences and then identify your preferred intelligences.

1. I am skilful in working with objects .... (0–5)

2. I have a good sense of direction ....

3. I have a natural ability to sort out arguments between friends ....

4. I can remember the words to music easily ....

5. I am able to explain topics which are difficult and make them clear ....

6. I always do things one step at a time ....

7. I know myself well and understand why I behave as I do ....

8. I enjoy community activities and social events ....

9. I learn well from talks, lectures and listening to others ....

10. When listening to music I experience changes in mood ....

11. I enjoy puzzles, crosswords, logical problems ....

12. Charts, diagrams, visual displays are important for my learning ....

13. I am sensitive to the moods and feelings of those around me ....

www.fultonpublishers.co.uk

14. I learn best when I have to get up and do it for myself ....

15. I need to see something in it for me before I want to learn something ....

16. I like privacy and quiet for working and thinking ....

17. I can pick out individual instruments in complex musical pieces ....

18. I can visualise remembered and constructed scenes easily ....

19. I have a well developed vocabulary and am expressive with it ....

20. I enjoy and value taking written notes ....

21. I have a good sense of balance and enjoy physical movement ....

22. I can discern pattern and relationships between experiences or things ....

23. In teams I cooperate and build on the ideas of others ....

24. I am observant and will often see things others miss ....

25. I get restless easily ....

26. I enjoy working or learning independently of others ....

27. I enjoy making music ....

28. I have a facility with numbers and mathematical problems ....

Multiple intelligences: key to statements

Intelligence		Statements				Total score
Linguistic	*your score*	5	9	19	20	
Mathematical and logical	*your score*	6	1	22	28	
Visual and spatial	*your score*	2	12	18	24	
Musical	*your score*	4	10	17	27	
Interpersonal	*your score*	3	8	13	23	
Intrapersonal	*your score*	7	15	16	26	
Kinaesthetic	*your score*	1	14	21	25	

www.fultonpublishers.co.uk

Activity 3.4
Implications of multiple intelligences

What would be the main teaching implications for a child with a similar balance of intelligences, as revealed in the intelligences activity (Activity 3.3)? Record your response below:

Main teaching implications

Activity 3.5
Designing activities to enhance the self-concept

Plan a series of six activities, with a class or subject teacher in your school, which are specifically designed to:

(a) enhance the self-concept; and
(b) encourage the development of an internal locus of control
  – for a pupil who experiences learning and/or behaviour problems.

Briefly describe those activities below:

The activities

1.	4.
2.	5.
3.	6.

www.fultonpublishers.co.uk

Objectives

This chapter has been designed to enable you to:

(a) identify strategies which enable pupils with special educational needs to make progress in literacy;
(b) advise and support colleagues in applying the strategies in the classroom.

Activity 4.1
Benefits and drawbacks of the literacy hour for children with special educational needs

In the space provided write down what you perceive to be the advantages of the literacy hour for pupils with special educational needs.

Advantages of the literacy hour

What do you perceive as the disadvantages of the literacy hour for pupils with SEN?

Disadvantages of the literacy hour

Activity 4.2
Deployment of the LSA within the literacy hour

List how your school deploys your learning support assistant.

During the literacy hour	Outside the literacy hour

www.fultonpublishers.co.uk

Objectives

Part Two of this book has been designed to enable you to:

- work in partnership with teachers, pupils, parents and associated professionals in order to analyse 'problem behaviour' from different perspectives;
- communicate effectively with a variety of people in one-to-one and small group settings;
- use effective negotiating skills;
- make effective presentations;
- monitor and evaluate the quality of special educational needs provision.

Part Two: Managing people – Activities

Objectives

Chapter 5 has been designed to enable you to:

(a) work in partnership with teachers, pupils, parents and associated professionals in order to analyse 'problem behaviour' from different perspectives;

(b) advise colleagues, pupils and parents about strategies which can be used to prevent and manage problem behaviours.

Chapter 5: Managing pupil behaviour – Activities

Activity 5.1
Perceptions of 'problem behaviour'

Examine critically a report about a child whose behaviour is considered to be problematic (or interview one of the child's teachers, or parent(s)/carers), in order to determine the kinds of causal factors which have been taken into account and those which have been omitted.

Summarise your findings below. (Please respect confidentiality – do not use the child's/school's real name in your notes.)

Types of 'causes' taken into account in a written or verbal account of a problem behaviour.

Types of 'causes' omitted.

---

www.fultonpublishers.co.uk

Activity 5.2
Factors associated with problem behaviour

With a teacher colleague, appraise the factors which appear to be associated with the problem behaviour of a particular child. Refer to Chapter 5 to ensure that you give adequate consideration to the range of causal factors. Try to be specific.

Factors associated with the 'problem' behaviour

Within the learner

Within the curriculum

Within the learning environment

---

www.fultonpublishers.co.uk

For the same pupil, consider factors within the 'learner', the 'curriculum' and the 'learning environment' that are associated with successful academic and/or social learning. Record your responses below. Try to be specific.

Factors associated with 'successful' learning outcomes (same pupil)

Within the learner

Within the curriculum

Within the learning environment

www.fultonpublishers.co.uk

Discuss the previous summaries with your colleague and list three actions which you and your colleagues could collectively make which could help to minimise the occurrence of the problem behaviour. Record your responses below.

Three actions which could minimise the occurrence of the problem behaviour

1.

2.

3.

Chapter 6: Communication skills – giving and receiving information – Activities

Objectives

Chapter 6 has been designed to enable you to:

(a) communicate effectively with colleagues, pupils, parents, governors and outside agencies in one-to-one and small group settings.

Activity 6.1
Who does a SENCO communicate with?

Consider your role:

Who do you communicate with?

Why do you communicate? What are the different purposes? Think of particular examples and then determine what the purpose was.

Examples	*Purposes*

---

www.fultonpublishers.co.uk

How do you communicate and in what ways?

Identify two tricky situations you have had to handle recently.

Activity 6.2
'Out talking your partner'

Try this activity and those which follow (if time permits) or try them as a follow-up exercise.

1. Form pairs, partners A and B.

2. Both partners A and B should speak at the same time to one another, for one minute, on the subject of 'My favourite meal'.

3. Did you manage to keep talking?

If not, was it because by talking you were unable to listen?

Activity 6.3
'Brick-walling'

1. Form (new) pairs, A and B.

2. Partner A is to speak to partner B for 1 minute on the subject of 'My ideal holiday'. Partner B remains seated and indicates that they are not listening.

3. After 1 minute reverse the procedure.

4. Afterwards, discuss (in your pairs)
   – as a listener, how did you 'brickwall'?
   – as a speaker, how did you feel?

    www.fultonpublishers.co.uk

Activity 6.4
Giving attention

1. Form new pairs, A and B.

2. Partner A to speak to partner B for 2 minutes on 'I've just won £5,000 – how I will spend it'. Partner B is to give attention but remain silent.

3. After 2 minutes reverse the procedure (B to speak to A).

4. Afterwards discuss:
   - how difficult/easy was it to say nothing in response? Did you convey attention by body language?
   - as a speaker did you feel heard? If so what made you feel heard? What kind of small, encouraging response might have helped?

Activity 6.5
Giving feedback

Work in groups of three

1. Person A should talk about a problem that they are dealing with at the moment. Be careful to choose something 'light' that you do not mind other people sharing !

2. Person B should practise active listening techniques, occasionally giving encouraging sounds or words. Person C should act as observer.

3. After 5 minutes Person B is to summarise beginning with 'It sounds as if...'

4. The observer should feedback his or her observations and the three people should swap roles, so that A or B take on the role of observer.

www.fultonpublishers.co.uk

Objectives

Chapter 7 has been designed to enable you to:

(a) use effective negotiating skills;
(b) give and receive criticism effectively;
(c) provide positive feedback.

*Chapter 7:
Communication
skills –
influencing others
– Activities*

Activity 7.1
Giving appropriate feedback

Work in small groups and discuss how you would give feedback in the following scenarios:

> 1. You recently tried to introduce a new project at a staff meeting. Most of the staff were initially quite receptive of the idea but one of the deputies was very negative. She was generally dismissive of what you had to say and made it clear that she thought the idea had no chance of success. You felt that this undermined your idea with the rest of the staff. What do you do?

> 2. A member of staff, who is in your department, has been on a course on differentiation and was supposed to feedback to the rest of the staff at a staff meeting. In spite of reminders he appears reluctant to do so. You have given plenty of opportunity for this but so far the issue seems to have been side-stepped. You decide to pin your colleague down to a date.

> 3. You are chairing an Annual Review for Emma, a child with specific learning difficulty. You have drawn up an agenda which began with the parents' contribution. Emma's father has held the floor for half an hour demanding extra county support for Emma and criticising the teaching provision. You have already consulted the staff and agreed with the support service that Emma's support should be retained but there is no need to increase it. Time is pressing and you are aware that you will not complete the agenda unless you can move on. What do you do?

> 4. Outline a difficult situation in which you are involved at present and discuss how you would give feedback.

Through the provision of positive feedback and constructive criticism people can attempt to 'influence' the professional practices (and other behaviours) of their colleagues, friends, relatives and peers.

Activity 7.2
Ways of influencing others

How do you attempt to influence other people? Study the ways in which people influence others as indicated in Chapter 7 and decide which strategies you use. In what ways might you want to change some of those strategies?

www.fultonpublishers.co.uk

Chapter 8: Communication skills – making presentations – Activities

Objectives

Chapter 8 has been designed to enable you to make effective presentations.

Activity 8.1
Identifying situations where you may make presentations

Presentation skills

What are the situations where you have to make presentations/make use of group management skills?

What factors result in successful presentations/group management?

What are some of the difficulties/difficult situations?

Activity 8.2
Delivering a presentation – verbal and non-verbal techniques

Work in groups of three

1. Person A will choose *one* aspect of verbal delivery and *one* aspect of body language. Make a brief presentation for 2 minutes on 'Why the school day should be shortened', concentrating particularly on using those two techniques.

2. At the end of the 2 minutes the group should discuss how successful those techniques were.

3. Change roles so that another person makes a presentation on 'Why the school day should be lengthened'. Evaluate in the same way.

4. Change roles again if time allows.

Activity 8.3
Dealing with difficult individuals

In groups of three

1. Briefly brainstorm the merits of devising Individual Education Plans (IEPs) for pupils with special educational needs.

2. Person A to make a brief presentation on 'The importance of IEPs'. Persons B and C will each respond as a different personality type. The whole presentation will last no longer than 5 minutes, so give person 'A' a chance to make some points.

3. Discuss how person A felt about these responses and the best way to respond to such a situation.

4. Change roles. The 'audience' should choose two different personality types. Repeat the process. If there is time, change roles again.

www.fultonpublishers.co.uk

Activity 8.4
Producing guidelines for making presentations

Your task is to produce some guidelines for colleagues on making presentations. Aim to make these guidelines as practical as possible. The following prompts may help you consider how to carry this out.

Section 1. Structuring your presentation

How to:

- structure your session
- begin a session
- end a session
- make the session interesting
- take account of limited attention spans
- ensure adequate breaks

Section 2. Producing clear aims which meet the audience's needs

How to ensure that:

- you have clear aims and objectives
- participants have positive expectations for the session
- people know why they are there / the purpose of the session
- people agree with the purpose of the session
- you have prepared the ground before the session
- you get feedback about the session
- you evaluate whether your aims have been achieved
- work from the session is followed up

Section 3: The physical environment

How to:

- choose the venue
- set out the room
- ensure physical needs of participants are met
- make the best use of your own staffroom
- use your own position in the room
- make the best use of equipment and visual aids
- support your presentation with written information

Section 4: Personal presentation skills

How to:

- make best use of non-verbal communication
- make the best use of your personal appearance
- make the best use of your voice
- communicate enthusiasm
- manage the nerves
- communicate humour – the great ice-breaker

      www.fultonpublishers.co.uk

Section 5: Group management

How to:

- get the attention of the group/get them quiet so you can start
- ensure the active involvement of the group
- organise groupwork
- get a quiet group to contribute
- deal with questions
- deal with a hostile audience
- ensure the whole group takes responsibility for the success of the session
- get people back from working groups
- deal with a group which never produces anything/reaches any agreement
- motivate a group who are bored
- work with staff who are tired
- ensure you have the right group size

Section 6: Dealing with difficult individuals

How to deal with the person who:

- moans and casts doom and gloom
- puts you on the spot with a difficult question
- does not contribute at all
- talks when you are talking
- asks hostile questions
- monopolises the discussion

Activity 8.5
Giving and receiving feedback

Use the structure provided in Appendix 4 ('Giving and receiving feedback') to give constructive feedback to the presenter of the previous activity (Activity 8.4).

Objectives

Chapter 9 has been designed to play a key role in monitoring and evaluating the quality of special educational needs provision which is made in your school.

Chapter 9:
Monitoring and
evaluation –
Activities

Activity 9.1
Characteristics of effective provision for 'special educational needs'

1. Working in pairs draw up a list of characteristics of effective special educational provision.

2. Join another 'pair' and share your lists, noting agreements and disagreements.

Characteristics of effective special educational provision

www.fultonpublishers.co.uk

Activity 9.2
Identifying monitoring and evaluating provision

With reference to the information obtained through Activity 9.1 decide which aspects of the management of special educational provision you should monitor and evaluate within the next school term.

Aspects of the management of special educational provision which should be monitored and evaluated in the next school term:

Activity 9.3
Monitoring aspects of teaching and learning

What aspects of teaching and learning should or could a SENCO monitor?

Hard data	Soft data
E.g. Test results	E.g. Attitudes

www.fultonpublishers.co.uk

Index